Shamanism

AS A SPIRITUAL PRACTICE
FOR DAILY LIFE

TOM COWAN

THE CROSSING PRESS
FREEDOM, CALIFORNIA

This book is dedicated to Tom Downes, Lorenza Menegoni,
Phyllis Curott, Rodger Parsons, and the Drum we used to
sit around in Brooklyn.

Many people helped bring this book into being. I wish to thank Susan Lee Cohen, my agent, for keeping faith in the project; Joy Oliveira Steltzner, Maura Shaw, Sarah Wiehe, and Cait Johnson for reading the manuscript and courageously making important suggestions; Brooke Isberg for making me tell her how the book was coming along; Linda Gunnarson, my editor, for taking on the project with great enthusiasm; Kathy Glass for her wise copyediting; Jack Maguire for daily help and for his own inspiring spiritual practice; and last but not least, Peg Elliot Mayo, who flicked a switch and there was light.

For information on bulk purchases or group discounts for this and other Crossing Press titles, please contact our Special Sales Manager at 800-777-1048.

Visit our Website on the Internet at: www.crossingpress.com

Library of Congress Cataloging-in-Publication Data
Cowan, Thomas Dale.
    Shamanism as a spiritual practice for daily life / by Tom Cowan.
        p. cm.
    ISBN 0-89594-838-9 (pbk.)
    1. New Age movement. 2. Shamanism. 3. Spiritual life--New Age movement I. Title.
BP605.N48C685   1996
299'.93--dc20   96-22341
                                                                                                        CIP

CONTENTS

PREFACE

A friend who is an authority on mystery traditions once asked me, "Why would anyone in his right mind want to learn shamanism at a weekend workshop?" She was thinking about the classic initiations into shamanism among tribal people in which, as she put it, "you're sitting quietly in your yurt, minding your own business, when suddenly a hideous four-headed spirit monster blasts its way through the door flap, grabs you by the neck, yanks you up through the smoke-hole into some dreary realm, where it proceeds to slap you around, rip you apart, dip you in a foul-smelling gook, staple you back together again, and drop you back through the smoke-hole. Then it says, 'There! Now you're a shaman!'"

I had to agree with her. If that's the initiation into shamanism, who needs it? It doesn't sound like a very pleasant way to spend a weekend, much less one you have to pay money for. Fortunately, this classic description of being introduced to shamanism, found in many indigenous cultures in some form or another, is not the only way. Consider the story of Aua, an Eskimo-Iglulik shaman.

At his birth, Aua was apparently lifeless, with the umbilical cord wrapped around his neck, but Ardjuaq, a shaman from a nearby village, predicted that the young baby, lying beside its mother, would become a great shaman. "He is born to die, but he shall live," she prophesied. Throughout his life, the boy's family strictly observed the appropriate rituals and taboos to assure his continued health and to prepare him to become a shaman. Aua grew to adulthood, married, had four children, and lived the life of an average man in his tribal community, hunting and fishing, but always observing the ancient rituals and lifeways proper for a candidate for shamanhood. But the calling eluded him.

Aua visited elder shamans, offered gifts, and beseeched them to train him, but to no avail. They gave his gifts away and left Aua on his own. As he explained, "I endeavored to become a shaman by the help of others; but in this I did not succeed." Frustrated, Aua eventually sought the silence and solitude of the wilderness, fell into a dark melancholy, wept copiously, and tried to understand the source of his perpetual unhappiness.

Then one day, something shifted. As Aua relates, "I felt a great, inexplicable joy, a joy so powerful that I could not restrain it, but had to break into song, a mighty song, with only room for the one word: joy, joy!" This was the turning point in Aua's spiritual journey. "In the midst of such a fit of mysterious and overwhelming delight I became a shaman, not knowing myself how it came about. But I was a shaman. I could see and hear in a totally different way. I had gained my enlightenment, the shaman-light of brain and body...I could see through the darkness of life!"

And the same light shone out from Aua, "imperceptible to human beings, but visible to all the spirits of earth and sky and sea, and these now came to me and became my helping spirits." He said, "I felt such a power of vision that I could see right through the house, in through the earth and up into the sky." To help him with these visions, Aua relied on his two primary spirits. One was a "shore spirit," whom he perceived as a small woman, "bright and cheerful" and resembling "a sweet little live doll...the length of a man's arm." The other was a shark, a rare creature in the waters near Aua's homeland. "These two, the shore spirit and the shark, were my principal helpers, and they could aid me in everything I wished." And to call them, he sang a song of few words: "Joy, joy, joy, joy!" [1]

The search for a spiritual practice can be confusing because ultimately we are seeking a path for the soul, and the soul's true journey through life often lies hidden in the shadowy landscape just beneath conscious awareness. As modern Westerners, we may have only a tenuous connection with our souls to begin with, since so much of our culture and way of life either ignores the soul's deepest longings or offers a hostile environment for nurturing an intimate relationship with the soul. We perceive glimpses, whispers, and slight intimations about our souls' vital needs, but we are often completely lost when it comes to finding the direction the soul needs to travel.

Many of us spend years stumbling through the darkness, searching for the light and joy of life. We blunder along, waiting for the light to shine, trying to remain faithful, open, and ready to respond. But in spite of all our efforts, the place, the timing, and the occasion of enlightenment are often determined by forces greater than our own.

On his journey from birth to shamanhood, Aua encountered many wrong turns, detours, and dead ends; yet he sensed throughout his long years of preparation and waiting that his true destiny was to walk the shaman's path. Aua is not unlike many men and women in other cultures, including our own, who recognize, sometimes early in life, sometimes later, a strong vocation or calling to lead a certain type of spiritual life in spite of numerous stumbling blocks that lie in the way. Worldly distractions, wrong advice, lack of support from others, and the unwillingness to make the necessary changes to lead a truly spiritual life prevent us for many years from finding our path. Then at some mysteriously proper moment, the sky brightens, and we see the truth: that we are on it. And like Aua, we are swept with joy.

Shaman is a Tungus word from Central Asia referring to a person who uses a state of spiritual excitement to enter the normally imperceptible realities of the spirit world to get help for him- or herself or others. But students of language disagree over the exact etymology of the word. Where does it come from? What was its original meaning? What ancient practices or rituals inspired this mysterious word *shaman*, which still has the power to make us tingle?

Among the early rootwords from which shaman may have been derived are words for "knowledge" and "heat"—two ideas that capture fully the rich traditions of classic shamanism and its modern counterparts. The shaman is someone on fire with certain kinds of knowledge that come from the spirit world. In any era, the practice of shamanism puts one on the path that leads to a growing awareness of the spiritual mysteries of the universe.

At the heart of shamanism are the controlled visionary experiences that connect the practitioner with the spiritual beings who guide, guard, instruct, and bless his or her life. In traditional shamanism these personal spirits are unique to each tribal culture; in modern core shamanism the spirits are personal and unique to each practitioner's private spiritual experience, background, and belief system.

The focus of this book is "core shamanism": the key elements of traditional, indigenous shamanism that are found worldwide and can be incorporated into one's daily life, similar to the way you might follow spiritual practices such as yoga, meditation, journal keeping, and prayer. Core shamanism as a spiritual practice does not require any specific religious beliefs, but it invariably encourages practitioners to discover animism: the ancient world view of our ancestors that all created things—humans, animals, plants, landscapes, elements, and seasons—have an intelligent, communicative life force or spirit. Most modern people have little familiarity with this view of the universe. But the chapters that follow will introduce you to this way of perceiving the natural world and suggest a program for developing a spiritual practice based on traditional shamanic techniques found in tribal cultures the world over.

Specifically, we will explore the exciting resurgence of shamanism in modern times (Chapter One), the vital role of animal spirits in the shaman's practice (Chapter Two), and classic methods for journeying into the lower and upper realms of the spirit world (Chapter Three).

Our connections with the Earth and the horizons and landscapes that encompass our daily lives are important in shamanic practice, so we will learn visionary techniques to meet, honor, and live with the spirits of nature and the physical world, whether we live in rural or urban settings (Chapters Four, Five, and Six).

As children we had spontaneous shamanic experiences, accompanied by a strong sense of oneness with the universe. These were our earliest mystical experiences, and we will consider ways to incorporate them into our adult practice of shamanism (Chapter Seven).

The spirits of ancestors and even more recently deceased relatives and friends play important instructional roles in shamanism, and we will discover time-honored methods for strengthening our spiritual links with those who have passed on into the next world (Chapter Eight).

Finally, we will consider ways to form and facilitate shamanic drumming circles, and look at some ideas for journeying into the Otherworld that can enrich our spiritual lives (Chapter Nine).

Not everyone who practices shamanism becomes a shaman, but anyone with an interest in, and dedication to, shamanic wisdom can become a shamanic practitioner—a man or woman like yourself who searches through the darkness of life for the spiritual path that is personal, creative, life-affirming, and joyful. I hope the chapters that follow will help you in your search for that path.

 CHAPTER ONE

RE-INVENTING SHAMANISM

One of the remarkable spiritual developments in our time is the growing desire among Western people to explore more ancient forms of spirituality that revere the Earth as a living, conscious entity. These older spiritual traditions often incorporate visionary techniques that allow us to participate with the spirits of nature on land, at sea, and in the sky. Contemporary men and women raised in the dominant culture are feeling a deep longing in the soul to rediscover the Earth-honoring values and customs of their distant tribal ancestors whose lives were rooted in the ecological realities of the natural world. People living thoroughly urbanized and technologized lives are seeking ways to reconnect with more ancient peoples who listened to the spirits of the natural world for instruction in ways to live in harmony and kinship with the Earth's various communities of life.

As if the Earth herself is responding favorably to these developments, there is emerging a form of shamanism accessible to Westerners that can unite these separate strains of soulful longing into a spiritual practice that blends ancient wisdom with contemporary life: modern shamanism.

As a practitioner of modern core shamanism, I am often asked how a millennia-old spiritual tradition that evolved in tribal cultures and emerged from animistic conceptions of nature can be adapted to modern men and women whose sensibilities have been shaped by urban life, complex technology, and the mainstream religions that tend either to ignore nature or to view it with suspicion. But for all the mysterious and exotic phenomena associated with shamanism, the core shamanic experience is really simple, timeless, and universal.

There are many ways to define and describe shamanism, which is basically a way of viewing reality and the use of empirical techniques to function within that view of reality. Following is a personal definition: *Shamanism is the intentional effort to develop intimate and lasting relationships with personal helping spirits by consciously leaving ordinary reality and journeying into the nonordinary realms of the spirit world.*

We will look at this definition in more detail in a moment. For now, we can use the story of Aua to illustrate the basic concept. The shaman's view of reality is that there are invisible worlds of spirit that lie beyond the physical earth and sky. The primary technique for functioning within that view of reality is the shamanic journey, which consists of various methods for altering the shaman's consciousness so that it can move outside ordinary space and time to explore the spiritual realms that most people encounter only in myth and dreams. Friendly spirit companions, such as Aua's shark and shore spirit, accompany shamans on these journeys and teach them how to make their visions of nonordinary, sacred reality a joyful but challenging mainstay of ordinary life. This is the core shamanic experience. It is not bound to any particular culture, continent, or century.

In spite of the rapid growth of interest in shamanism in North America over the last generation, the possibility of Westerners living a spiritual life based on animistic beliefs and rituals that developed in tribal cultures may still seem strange. How can middle-class Americans, most likely raised in one of the mainstream religions of the twentieth century, follow a spiritual path that seems so remote from the cultural context in which they live their daily lives? Would we not have to travel to isolated tribal communities where shamanistic practices have survived and find a traditional shaman willing to accept us as apprentices?

And would the training not take long years of rigorous practice and instruction?

AN ANALOGY FROM THE FAR EAST

To understand these objections and their resolutions, it may be helpful to consider, as an analogy, the history of Zen Buddhism in the West. One hundred fifty years ago, we might have raised the same questions to an American who said he was planning to practice *any* form of Buddhism. Would he not have to travel to the Far East, join a monastery where monks would be willing to take him on as a student, and would it not take years and years of intense study and practice to become a monk himself? The answer at that time would have been yes. In the mid-nineteenth century very few Americans—with the exceptions of Emerson, Thoreau, Fuller, and other New England Transcendentalists—were familiar with Buddhism in any of its forms, and the likelihood of meeting and studying with a Zen monk or any other kind of Buddhist monk in the United States was nil.

All that changed in the early twentieth century. Through efforts of D. T. Suzuki (and others), Zen practice was introduced to the United States. Zen teachers immigrated, Zen centers were established, eventually a handful of Americans went to Japan to study and returned to teach, and gradually Americans became familiar with Zen practice. Today, almost seventy years or three generations later, Zen has adapted to American culture to such an extent that many proponents and practitioners look upon their practice as constituting an American brand of Zen Buddhism.

But this should not surprise us, for this has been the history of Buddhism in general since its beginning some 2500 years ago. Because of its resiliency and universal message, Buddhism adapts to the countries where it is introduced. Today there are Tibetan, Korean, Chinese, Japanese, and other cultural expressions of Buddha's teachings and practices. It was only a matter of time before American forms of Buddhism evolved.

Some of the cultural adaptations that we can see in American Zen Buddhism stem directly from American culture in the twentieth century. For example, here the term "monk" can designate either a man or woman, unlike in the East, where men become monks and women become nuns. American Buddhism has introduced the concept of "Zen practitioner" to mean a lay student of Buddhism who, in some Zen centers, has equal training with monks, but who continues to live in the world outside the monastery. Administrative structures for Zen communities are often less hierarchical and more democratic, as we might expect in a community composed primarily of Americans.

The story of Zen Buddhism in the West is becoming the story of shamanism.

SHAMANISM IN MODERN AMERICAN CULTURE

Michael Harner has done for shamanism what D. T. Suzuki did for Buddhism. He introduced shamanism to mainstream Americans. Trained as an anthropologist with extensive fieldwork among the Jívaro and Conibo people of South America in the mid-1950s, Harner was accepted by local shamans and introduced to their methods of healing and their spiritual perceptions of reality. In time, backed by continued research, personal practice, and firsthand study of other shamanic traditions, Harner discovered a solid core of shamanic practices that were widespread among indigenous cultures. In the 1970s, intrigued by the notion that if shamanism were truly a universal human ability it could be practiced by mainstream Americans, Harner began teaching a few friends and students the shamanic techniques for seeing and journeying into the spirit world.

The results were surprising. His earliest students discovered their ability to practice shamanism so quickly and easily that they often commented that it was like remembering something they didn't know they knew. Now, a generation later, Harner himself continues to be amazed at how easily Westerners can learn the basic techniques of the shamanic journey into the spirit world of nonordinary reality.

In the early 1980s Harner took the bold step of creating the Foundation for Shamanic Studies (originally called the Center for Shamanic Studies) to offer an extensive program of training courses in core shamanic practices. Today, the Foundation teaches worldwide, even among indigenous people who have invited instructors from the Foundation to revitalize or re-introduce basic shamanic techniques. In many cases, these invitations come from tribal societies that have lost many of their traditions due to the influence of Christianity and scientific rationalism, both of which have historically taken a dim view of native spiritual practices everywhere.

Harner's methods of teaching and practicing shamanism have been acknowledged over the years as based on solid spiritual and healing principles authentic to the classical shamanism found among indigenous peoples. These practices are extremely effective in transforming and enriching peoples' lives physically, emotionally, and spiritually. But perhaps the most dramatic validation came in the summer of 1993 when ten shamanic practitioners from the United States and Europe, sponsored by the Foundation for Shamanic Studies, were invited to Tuva, a new republic situated between Mongolia and Siberia that was formed after the breakup of the former Soviet Union.

In spite of Stalin's purges of shamans, and the Communists' attempts to eradicate spiritual practices of every form from the Soviet Union—for example, making it illegal to own a drum—a few shamans defiantly continued the old ways, practiced in secret, and preserved the spiritual and healing traditions of their ancestors. They kept their drums even at the risk of being put to death. In 1993, at the request of the Tuvan government, Western shamanic practitioners met with these traditional shamans to share knowledge, do ritual, and explore each other's shamanic practices. It was a remarkable week. Not only were Western shamanic practitioners accepted by Siberian shamans as equals, the Westerners performed impressive healing work on local people, including native shamans. Tuvans and Westerners understood each other and participated together in shamanic ceremonies because both groups operated out of the same principles and basic practices.

A curious incident that occurred on the Tuvan expedition validated core shamanism in a rather humorous way. One of the participants left his rattle in the hotel room when they departed for the day and didn't realize this until the group was already out in the countryside. Later when called upon to do some shamanic work, he found himself without a rattle. However, in his pocket, courtesy of the lifestyle and technology of the West, was a small plastic box of Tic-Tac breath mints. He pulled out the plastic box and shook it, and it worked. The efficacy of core shamanism, in this case the technique of using rattling sounds to assist the alteration of consciousness, was clearly demonstrated in the land where the word *shaman* originated: the heart of Central Asia.

A similar lesson came home to me a few years ago when I was the faculty coordinator for a shamanic studies week at a holistic learning center. A Korean and a Guatemalan shaman were among the faculty participants. During the faculty orientation, the two got into a friendly but competitive discussion over the powers of their respective drums. The Korean shaman emphasized the importance of deerskin for the drum, while the Guatemalan shaman spoke of the virtues and strengths of jaguar skin. Had I been trained in Korean or Guatemalan shamanism, I'm sure I would have taken sides accordingly, but I sat back, enjoyed the conversation, and resisted the temptation to reach into my drum bag and whip out my Remo hand drum made of DuPont Mylar® polyester film, a plastic material popularized by Mickey Hart, the former drummer of the Grateful Dead. It cost $19.95 at Drummers' World. There is a lot to be said for Mylar®. For one thing, it doesn't loosen up in humid weather, like animal skin, which makes the drum sound "thwocky" and in some cases, totally unusable. Mylar's® primary virtue is reliability. I think I could have argued my case very eloquently, but I'm sure I would not have convinced the Korean and the Guatemalan shamans to go Mylar®.

It is important to honor and abide by the traditions of indigenous shamanic practices if you are trained in them and they are what you practice. Core shamanism, however, can adapt the basic principles and general practices to situations that transcend any particular culture's traditions. I do have a drum made from the skin of an animal whose spirit I honor whenever I use it. But as a practitioner of core shamanism, I am not limited to using only that drum, particularly on wet, rainy nights when I have no fire to tighten it up.

SHAMANS AND SHAMANIC PRACTITIONERS

In the winter of 1982–83 I was introduced to shamanic practices by Michael Harner during an intensive three days exploring core shamanism. Like many people, I was immediately drawn to the shamanic journey as a safe, rejuvenating way of discovering realities that I had long suspected existed but that I had no way of accessing. Journeying rekindled my childhood instincts that there were spirits in nature, that "wonderlands" existed just beneath the surface of the earth, that the faery realms I had read and fantasized so much about in my youth really could be entered and explored. I came away from that training determined to continue journeying, and serendipitously, within a few weeks I discovered a small group of men and women who met weekly to practice shamanism. As if the spirits were watching over my development, the group met weekly in a Brooklyn brownstone only a twenty-minute walk from where I lived at the time. To this day I must credit what I learned from that group of shamanic practitioners—and the spirits who taught us all—as being among the most valuable shamanic training I have received.

Shamanism as a spiritual practice for contemporary men and women is not about becoming a shaman. This book is not a handbook for training shamans. It will, however, provide the basic information and techniques for *practicing* shamanism—for becoming a shamanic practitioner, or what we might call a student of experiential shamanism. In fact, I prefer to reserve the term *shaman* for people trained in the traditional methods of shamanism that are unique to indigenous tribes and cultures. Shamans might be native men and women fortunate enough to live in traditional communities where shamanism has survived as a vital spiritual and healing tradition. Or the term *shaman* could be applied to Westerners who have been apprenticed to native shamans and trained extensively in the old ways of their people.

Traditional pathways to becoming a shaman vary from culture to culture and even within a culture. Americo Yabar, a Q'ero shaman in the Andes, explained that to be initiated as a shaman in his culture always requires a transmission that "can come from lightning, from a master who determines you are ready, or from a feeling inside yourself that you have been called to that path as a vocation. All three paths are strange and difficult." [1]

A shamanic practitioner need not consider himself or herself a shaman. A practitioner is, quite simply, someone who practices. A practice is something that one does with regularity, consistency, and a strong desire for improvement. Whether one eventually acquires the skills and powers of a shaman and becomes capable of performing the same healing services for others that shamans perform for their tribal communities is not our concern. If it happens, fine; it is the result of the spirits accepting us and using us as channels for healing. If it does not happen, the commitment to shamanic practice is rewarding and valuable in itself. Shamanism is a spiritual path worth walking for one's own personal development, as well as for the benefit of the nonhuman communities with which we share the planet.

Since shamanism is both a spiritual practice as well as a philosophy and system of healing, we should be clear from the start how these two are related to each other and how they factor into our commitments. This book, as its title indicates, is primarily about the former: shamanism as a spiritual practice. Even in tribal settings, the spiritual practice precedes the ability to heal because the rationale for illness and healing in tribal cultures is fundamentally spiritual. At the root of disease, illness, accidents, and general misfortune is the loss of one's spiritual power, and at the root of shamanic healing procedures is the reunion with spiritual power. The quality of life in tribal cultures, both individually and collectively, depends on communion with the world of spirits. Shamans, therefore, in order to be effective healers, must have strong personal relationships with helping spirits. It is not unusual, as the expedition to Tuva demonstrated, for modern practitioners of shamanism to acquire the same healing skills and abilities as tribal shamans, for ultimately the real healers are not the shamans but the spirits. The shaman or the shamanic practitioner functions as a conduit or channeler of spiritual energy and power received from his or her personal allies in the spirit world.

PRACTICING CORE SHAMANISM

Shamanism is the intentional effort to develop ongoing relationships with personal helping spirits by journeying into realms where the spirits dwell. Let's look at some of the implications of this definition.

First, shamanism is a way of perceiving the nature of the universe in a way that incorporates the normally invisible world of spirit. Shamans have different terms and phrases for this nonordinary reality, but most of them clearly imply that it is the realm where the spirits of the land and the animals, deceased ancestors, the gods and goddesses, and other spiritual entities dwell.

Second, shamans employ methods for altering consciousness so that they can send their spirits or souls—what many Westerners prefer to call consciousness—into the nonordinary reality of the spirit world to have direct experiences with particular spirits who become their friends, guides, guardians, instructors, and allies. These helping spirits might be the spirits of nature, animals, plants, the elements, ancestors, gods, goddesses, or teachers from various religious traditions. The act of sending one's consciousness into the spirit world is called the shamanic journey, and it allows the journeyer to view life and life's problems from a detached, spiritual perspective, not easily achieved in a state of ordinary consciousness. One of the most universal methods for altering consciousness for this spirit journey is a persistent, mesmerizing drumbeat.

Third, the reason for acquiring and nurturing ongoing personal relationships with helping spirits is to gain knowledge, wisdom, practical healing methods, and other vital information that can be brought back for one's own personal benefit or the benefit of others in the community.

In tribal cultures, shamans serve as healers, spiritual advisors, diviners, conductors of souls into the land of the dead, herbalists, dream interpreters, ceremonialists, storytellers, and keepers of the folk memory. These "shamanic services" are secondary to and dependent upon the shaman's spiritual practice, for any power or skill for doing these things well is attributed to the shaman's relationship with his or her helping spirits. Clearly, one does not have to be a shaman or rely upon helping spirits to interpret dreams, prescribe healing herbs, lead ceremonies, or tell stories. If a person performs these activities without the help of spirit allies, then they are merely human services, not invested with the spiritual power that derives from shamanism. What distinguishes the shaman's ability to do these things is the shaman's intense relationship with helping spirits and the knowledge of how to proceed that is received from those spirit helpers. At the heart of a shaman's power and reputation, therefore, is his or her spiritual practice.

The shaman is not the only one in the community who has visions and spirit helpers. In animistic societies most people participate in visionary activities that involve contacting and communing with spirits, such as vision quests, fasts, sweat ceremonies, night vigils, or extended periods of dancing and chanting during which participants unite with their personal spirits. Most people maintain ongoing relationships with their helping spirits throughout their lives by these means. What distinguishes the shaman from others is the intensity, seriousness, dedication, and calling to this aspect of life which far outweighs those of others in the tribe. In this respect, shamans are not unlike monks, ministers, and mystics in other religious traditions who may be engaged in the same spiritual practices as average men and women, but who have dedicated their lives to those practices and perform them with more rigor and devotion, often out of a profound sense of calling or vocation.

In recent years many Westerners have been having spontaneous shamanic experiences, much like the ones described by tribal people. Intelligent animals appear in dreams or physical reality; voices come from the wind or streams with clear messages; strange beings appear, apparently from nonterrestrial realms; the spirits of the deceased visit the living with instructions or requests; serious illness awakens a person to the need for a more spiritual way of living; near-death experiences completely shatter people's paradigms of reality and reorient their lives in more altruistic ways. There is a serious need for people trained in shamanic knowledge to help those who have these kinds of experiences understand their ramifications. Too often unsuspecting individuals think they are going crazy, hallucinating, or being possessed by demons when such occurrences take place. In a tribal culture, they would go to elders, wise in shamanic wisdom, who would help them interpret these incidents as possible initiatory crises leading to spiritual growth. In our culture, we go to therapists who psychologize or pathologize the nonordinary experience, or to the clergy, who may demonize it.

Over the years of practicing core shamanism both for personal spiritual reasons and as a healing service for others, I have met countless men and women who have used these kinds of experiences as an entry into shamanism. For many of them, shamanism has become their primary spiritual practice. They are not interested in being healers, diviners, or spiritual counselors for others, although they often find themselves thrown into that role when family members and friends, knowing about their practice, come to them for assistance. Sometimes shamanism replaces the religious traditions they were brought up in; for others, shamanism serves as an adjunct spiritual practice that deepens their religion, making it more immediate, personal, heartfelt, and Earth-centered. Either way, the primary role that core shamanism plays in their lives is that of a spiritual practice.

Modern shamanic practitioners have often walked several spiritual paths and undertaken many sacred journeys to reach the current point in their spiritual development. They have been "pioneers of the sacred," in that in the absence of extensive, firsthand instruction from indigenous shamans, they have created their spiritual practices from information gleaned from reading the literature on shamanism, from workshops with teachers of shamanism, and most important, from the advice and instruction of their own helping spirits. These practitioners have been on the cutting edge of developing an American brand of shamanism that honors our notions of independence, eclecticism, self-expression, and pragmatism, and that finds ways to temper American traits that tend to undermine shamanic thinking, such as excessive rationalism, materialism, mindless consumerism, and the unrelenting need for management and control. Ideally, we will forge a shamanism suited to life in modern America that draws on what is best in our society while it reforms those areas harmful to the human spirit and the health of the planet.

Shamanism everywhere is concerned with the health of the planet and its many species of inhabitants: animal, vegetable, mineral, and human. We are living in a time when the planet's health is in a precarious state due to human interference. The Earth's condition in future decades can be greatly improved by spiritual practices that adapt the ancient shamanic rituals of our ancestors and preserve the sacred knowledge of indigenous people who have lived harmoniously with nature for thousands of years. Yet no one is suggesting that we forsake modern life completely and return to the land—"go native" as some say—and place our hopes in a romantic primitivism that would inevitably prove unsatisfying and unlivable for people molded by modern Western sensibilities. We are not trying to create a tribe of "Wannabes," a term coined to refer to non-natives who have adopted tribal customs from indigenous peoples around the world in a misguided effort to regain a more Earth-centered form of spirituality. What is needed is a viable way to adapt the core elements of shamanism to the modern world and re-invent shamanism as a method of strengthening our commitment to the health and well-being of ourselves, other species, and the planet itself. But to do so means to find in shamanism a spiritual practice that will support and enrich our spiritual journeys through life, for life is our greatest gift, and life is the sacred journey that leads us home.

WHERE ARE OUR ROOTS?

Western civilization has known both roots and routes. From its source deep in ancient European traditions, the West as a culture has been greatly nurtured periodically by the values and vitality of people from other quarters of the globe. The "West" is a rich cultural mosaic from many races and traditions. No matter where we have come from, or what routes our journeys have taken, if we trace our ancestors back far enough, we find they were tribal people sitting around fires, singing, sharing sacred stories and dreams, and honoring the divine spirits upon whom they relied for life. Whether or not we are descended from European ancestry, if we were educated in the European-based traditions taught in Western schools, we can tap into the vestiges of European shamanic practices that have survived in Western folk traditions, faery legends, magical practices, and Earth-centered spiritual customs that we often encountered as children in faery and folk tales.

It is important for Westerners who hope to use shamanism as a spiritual practice to recognize and honor the shamanistic knowledge of the West for several reasons. First, if there is any truth to the notion of genetic memory, many of us have innate knowledge of shamanic practices buried deep within our psyches. Learning shamanism can often be the experience of releasing, remembering, and reapplying ancestral knowledge that has lain dormant throughout most of our lives. Perhaps this is why teachers of core shamanism discover the ready willingness and facility with which our students learn to practice shamanism. Perhaps this is why so many European-Americans, when learning how to practice shamanism for the very first time, say that they feel like they have finally "come home."

Second, the need to discover one's personal roots—in this case, spiritual roots—runs deep in people of all races and cultures. Too often, Americans reject their European pasts in the misguided effort to prove their "Americanism" or to safeguard themselves from what they perceive as Old World degeneracy, superstition, and corruption. But such efforts can be psychologically unhealthy, producing a race of people cut off from their past, drifting through the crises of modern life with a very short-term memory. Wisdom to meet the needs of the future must be drawn from an ancient well much deeper than the relatively shallow waters of the United States of America's roughly two hundred years of existence. For many reasons, discovering and using the shamanism indigenous to western Europe will strengthen our spiritual lives in general, and our shamanic practice in particular.

Third, we should be hesitant to adopt specific ceremonies and spiritual practices from contemporary native cultures and assume that we can make them our own. This has become an unfortunate trend in the United States, where many New Agers take the attitude that all native customs are up for grabs. Most attempts at this are a form of cultural imperialism, not unlike commandeering land and resources from native peoples. Ripping off spiritual practices is analogous to ripping off forests, meadows, and wildlife. Also, we would be naive to think that practices which require unique natural environments, specific theological assumptions, and the social support found only in many-thousand-year-old tribal cultures can be uprooted and transplanted to urban settings without losing their efficacy and the vital influence of the local land spirits upon whom that efficacy depends.

Only with extreme care and sensitivity to the spiritual integrity of native peoples do we dare to adapt their spiritual traditions. I would argue that doing so requires training and permission from the elders of those traditions. This is especially true in the case of spiritual customs that are not widespread among other cultures (i.e., are not among the core shamanic practices) and that are so intimately interwoven into a particular people's way of life that any attempt to lift those customs out of the cultural and theological matrix that makes them sacred would be an act of desecration.

But there are many ancient spiritual practices for which no culture or tribe can claim a monopoly. For example, consider the simple act of casting a circle of sacred space in which to do spiritual work. We will look at ways to do this more fully in a later chapter, but for now it is sufficient just to note that although core shamanism says very little specifically about how to construct a sacred circle, people who practice shamanism feel naturally inclined to create a special area in which to work by honoring the cardinal directions and the various spirits and powers that dwell in those directions. Certainly there is evidence that people all over the globe have used the circle as an ideal form in which to pray and do ritual. Too often, however, many of us adapt Native American customs for invoking the directions without fully understanding or appreciating the sacredness of these procedures, rather than develop our own formats for invoking the directions and creating a circle. In the spirit of core shamanism, we should not adopt or adapt other traditions mindlessly, but attempt to create our own methods, drawing on other cultures for inspiration. This can often be a hard call to make.

In spite of these warnings, we should keep in mind that many spiritual practices, both ancient and modern, transcend cultural boundaries. Fasting, sweating, vision quests, drumming and rattling, chanting, dancing, encountering helpful animal spirits, as well as working with the elements of earth, air, fire, and water are just some of the cross-cultural phenomena which, like certain songs and stories, are shared by many peoples and are adaptable to a wide range of social and ecological settings.

The history of religion is the history of cultural and theological borrowings. Christianity grew out of and adapted Jewish prayers and practices; Catholics sing Martin Luther's hymn "A Mighty Fortress Is Our God"; Christians, Wiccans, and other Neo-Pagans share the lively song "The Lord of the Dance"; some Native American shamans, raised in Christian denominations, number Jesus and Mary among their helping spirits.

Fourth, many Westerners do not want to forsake the religious traditions in which they were raised. Shamanism does not require this. Core shamanism is not a religion, but a spiritual practice. Core shamanism can build on and strengthen our spiritual fervor no matter what religion we belong to. Revitalizing European shamanic traditions can reinforce one's primary religious beliefs and practices, especially if they too derive from European sources.

So for these and other reasons that will become apparent as we proceed, we would do well to consider the shamanic principles and practices that have survived in European folk traditions and weave them into our spiritual practice whenever possible and appropriate. There is much that can be reclaimed from Western tribal and village cultures—and *should* be reclaimed because here lie the roots of Western civilization, which so desperately needs to reclaim its ancient sacred knowledge.

WHAT IS A SPIRITUAL PRACTICE?

As we already noted, a practice is quite simply something that one does. It can include sports, music, art, crafts, as well as spirituality. In addition to being something one does, the word *practice* also suggests regular repetition in the quest for improvement. One literally *practices* a practice.

Spiritual practices, regardless of the specific religion they grow out of, often share much in common: prayer, meditation, reading, study, support from other devotees, and the need for advice and direction from spiritual counselors. A spiritual practice also incorporates rituals and ceremonial activities, some of which are unique to specific religious traditions, while others are truly cross-cultural, found in and shared by more than one religion. These include fasting, making pilgrimages to holy sites, keeping vigils, lighting candles or sacred fires, burning herbs and incense, maintaining altars and shrines, engaging in various ascetic practices, and utilizing sacred tools or objects that may be specific to each tradition.

A spiritual practitioner commits himself or herself to performing these activities with dedicated regularity: some practices will be done daily, others weekly, monthly, or seasonally, and a few practices only on special occasions when the practitioner feels ready or called to do them. What is important for a practice is the commitment to pursue a spiritual path and walk it faithfully, incorporating some elements of it into one's life on a regular, if not daily, basis.

The spiritual practice of shamanism requires similar activities that grow out of the fundamental commitment to develop and nurture personal relationships with spirits and the spirit world. The basic practice is the shamanic journey, accompanied by ritual chanting or dancing to drums or rattles. Drumming, rattling, dancing, and chanting are activities which, in time, become so closely associated with the shamanic journey and communion with helping spirits that practitioners benefit from engaging in them for their own sake, even when there is not time or inclination for journeying into the spirit world.

In addition to the shamanic journey, most ritual activities that honor the spirits of nature, the elements, animals, plants, seasons, and the deceased are appropriate for shamanic practice, including the creation and maintenance of altars and sacred sites, either indoors or outside, that may be the setting for these rituals. Reading about and studying shamanism and other animistic spiritual customs will also enrich one's practice, but as we noted above, we must be ever mindful of the ethical (as well as the efficacious) considerations in borrowing or adapting sacred customs.

Although a spiritual practice can be intensely private—a kind of hermitage in which one prays and worships alone—most people need human support and encouragement. Actually, even hermits have recourse to spiritual confessors and directors, sometimes on a periodic basis. For shamanic practitioners a drumming group is the most effective method for receiving support and sharing experiences. A drumming group can be as few as three or four, or as many as ten or twelve people, as space permits, who meet for drumming and journeying.

Groups can meet once a week, twice a month, once a month, or as often as the members choose. Occasionally the group might get together to celebrate seasonal holy days or perform other rituals, possibly for healing.

I also recommend the ancient Irish custom of having a "soul friend." This practice, found in the early Irish church, is most likely based on even older druidic or shamanistic customs for nurturing the spirit. The key idea is that each of us—especially since we are engaged in private visionary work—needs a personal friend with whom we can confide the joys, sorrows, challenges, and struggles of the spiritual life. In the early Irish church a soul friend could be a monk, nun, priest, or lay person, either a man or woman, even someone younger in age. The important point was not the social or ecclesiastical status of the soul friend but that the person was indeed a "friend of your soul," someone who knew you and understood your spiritual aspirations, and someone you respected for her or his advice and insight into spiritual matters.

Following a custom found in many contemporary Buddhist centers, shamanic practitioners might also develop an art practice, a body practice, an academic practice, and a daily life practice to establish shamanism more solidly in their lives. Basically, each of these requires the practitioner to use his or her interest in shamanism as a theme or topic for artistic, athletic, and intellectual pursuits.

A shamanic art practice, for example, might include making or decorating drums and rattles, sketching or painting scenes and experiences from shamanic journeys, writing poetry based on journeys, and learning to play spontaneous "spirit" songs on simple instruments, such as flutes. A body practice can include any outdoor athletic activity that brings the practitioner closer to the spirits of nature (such as hiking, camping, mountain climbing, canoeing), or jogging, bicycling, and swimming in the presence of power animals. Academic practice simply means reading and studying about shamanism. The tremendous volume of books and articles published on shamanism in recent years makes this easy to do.

Daily life practice means weaving some shamanistic activity into your life on a daily basis. The following chapters contain various ways of doing this that include prayer, song, invocation, or ritual, reinforcing in us what David Suzuki and Peter Knudtson call the "Native Mind" in their fine book *Wisdom of the Elders: Honoring Sacred Native Visions of Nature.* The Native Mind sees all life as inherently holy; is not concerned with exerting dominion over nature; recognizes a Divine Being who permeates the cosmos and sanctifies it; heartily accepts responsibility for living harmoniously with the earth; makes sacrifices; expresses gratitude; sees the universe and everything in it as alive, dynamic, and changing yet animated by some unifying life force; understands the circular nature of time; accepts the mysteries of life; finds kinship and empathy with all creatures; and finally, the Native Mind celebrates joyfully its personal life and the Greater Life of which it is an integral part.[2]

Keeping a journal is a common spiritual practice for many people. Some people write their meditations or prayers as they are doing them; others use a journal to monitor and record the movements of their souls and to reflect on life's occurrences from a spiritual perspective. Shamanic practitioners can also use a journal to record journeys, dreams, and synchronicities. Our psychic, spiritual lives are holistic, not compartmentalized like so much of our ordinary lives. Our egos may fragment daily experiences, but the pieces come together again in nonordinary states of consciousness. A journal will help us see this.

WALKING SANELY BETWEEN THE WORLDS

Maintaining a healthy spiritual practice requires a sane balance between what in the West we like to call "the sacred and the profane." Western rationalism, based on a penchant for emphasizing the duality of experience, has widened the gap between the sacred and the nonsacred in ways that would have bewildered our ancestors, who found all life experience to be a finely woven tapestry that was considered sacred. In most tribal cultures the concept of profane was relegated to those few objects or people not officially dedicated or initiated—transformed—for some specific religious purpose or activity. For the most part, our earliest ancestors bequeathed to us a deep spiritual heritage in which all of creation is sacred and all activities can and should be performed in a sacred way.

Nevertheless, modern society forces us into many daily responsibilities that seem less than sacred but are necessary to maintain life, prosperity, and social standing in our communities. Unfortunately our severely compartmentalized lives are fast, furious, and fretful, filled with requirements that often leave little or no room for extensive spiritual practices. For the vast majority of Westerners, the sacred has been relegated to a few hours of official religious activities on one or two days of the week.

This being the case, we need to carefully and intelligently weave our spiritual activities into our broader secular lives to the extent we are each individually capable. We must become true walkers-between-the-worlds with a solid grounding in the worlds of ordinary and nonordinary realities. We must "walk in balance" on several levels, not the least of which is to balance successfully the unrelenting demands of everyday life: our families, friends, jobs, and social commitments. It would be unfortunate if our shamanic practice drove a wedge between us and the people in our lives who do not share our visions or spiritual interests. This can happen more easily than we might imagine. Many shamanic practitioners remain "in the closet" to family, friends, and fellow workers for fear of losing the respect of important people in their lives who would take a dim view of shamanism.

On the other hand, we must be mindful not to let a hostile culture weaken or undermine our beliefs in visionary experiences. We must strengthen and safeguard our commitment to beliefs considered by the dominant culture to be "primitive" or "pagan" in the negative sense of those terms, and not allow ourselves to be intimidated into giving up what we know, believe in, and feel called to practice. Practicing shamanism requires a sensitivity for knowing how wide to open the closet door, when to let others look in, and when, if at all, to invite someone to join you. At the present moment in history, not everyone has the freedom to step out of their spiritual closet and live as openly as they would like.

So for reasons of psychological and emotional health, we should strive to strike the right balance between ordinary and nonordinary reality, knowing what each requires, allocating the proper amount of time to each so that we continue to function in both worlds effectively. This was and is true of tribal shamans also. Although Western anthropologists and ethnographers first "diagnosed" all shamans as crazy—because they claimed to talk with trees, leave their bodies, journey into the spirit world, and shapeshift into animals—it soon became clear that if they were crazy, it didn't interfere with their functioning in daily life nor with their reputations! Shamans are among the most admired and respected people in their communities, both for their spiritual services and for the ordinary tasks of village life in which they engage just like everyone else. In fact, tribal people know perfectly well who the psychotics are in their villages. They are those individuals who cannot control their visionary experiences, can't "turn off" the voices they heard from the spirit world, can't distinguish between ordinary and nonordinary realities—people who spend *all* their time talking to trees and never to their own families. If shamans lose their grounding in ordinary reality and their ability to control visionary experiences, not only do they no longer function in daily life, but they are of no use as shamans. Being an effective shaman or shamanic practitioner requires being able to walk between the worlds, know their individual geographies, and not fall off the bridges between the worlds. If we drown in a deluge of private visionary experiences, we are of no use to others or ourselves.

We must also be prepared to accept the responsibilities that shamanic practice brings. When we allow the spirits a more active role in our lives, our lives change. You may find that you can no longer tolerate what many of your acquaintances take for granted. Addictions, abusive treatment of others, employment that is harmful to the good of the whole, even the self-destructive behavior of our closest friends—all these may force us into making radical changes in our lives. We must also go to the assistance of other shamanic practitioners when they are in need or look to us for guidance.

Finally, we must be ready to face what Christian mystics call the "dark night of the soul," those periods when our spiritual practice is not satisfying, when we feel abandoned by even our most helpful spirits, when self-doubts tell us that none of what we do makes any sense. This kind of despondency is terrifying even in mainstream spiritual traditions where there are plenty of others to go to for help and encouragement. Even more devastating are the dark nights of the soul for someone following a spiritual path that is not understood by most people in our culture.

And yet in spite of these warnings, the challenge to unite the sacred and "nonsacred" aspects of our lives in a shamanically meaningful way can be a great adventure. We live in a materialistic, agnostic culture where those who are not sure what they believe substitute faith in material possessions to give their lives solidity, and those who do know what they believe become intolerant and suspicious of others who believe differently. Perhaps this is the darkness of life that urgently needs illumination: the shadowy landscape of intolerance, bigotry, consumerism, and heartless entertainment, all tending to smother the soul's eternal flame. Shamanic practice can keep that flame burning brightly and light up the contemporary landscape.

Long-term practitioners of shamanism, when asked what they have learned or how they have changed because of their practice, overwhelmingly answer that they are no longer afraid of the universe, and they no longer feel isolated and alone. Instead they feel at home in nature and the greater universe; they know in their hearts that creation is sacred, joyful, and infused with divinity. In varying degrees they come to concur with the message from the Great Being of Strength that the Arctic people call Sila. Najagneg, an Eskimo shaman, told the Danish explorer Knud Rasmussen that Sila, "the soul of the universe,...(has) a voice so fine and gentle that even children cannot become afraid. What he says is: Be not afraid of the universe."[3]

 CHAPTER TWO

POWER ANIMALS

In many of the world's stories concerning the creation of the Earth, there is a brief period when humans and animals share the same language. At some point, through a mishap, vice, or some unfortunate act of human frailty, a Fall from this condition occurs; and from that point on, animals and human beings go their separate ways, no longer able to communicate. But in many cultures a few privileged individuals are exceptions to this, and through transformative experiences a few people regain knowledge of interspecies communication. They talk to animals, trees, rivers, and the stars. The shaman is one of these fortunate men and women, who, as the Celts say of druids and poets, learn to speak "the magical language of the birds."

The conditions of the Paradisal Age are accessible to the shaman because in an ecstatic trance the shaman's soul or spirit journeys outside ordinary time and space, where it enters the spiritual cosmos in which humans and animals can still speak to one another. In fact, being on friendly terms with animal spirits is a hallmark of the shaman's ability to transcend the current human predicament and re-enter a state similar to the Original Paradise from which humanity fell at the dawn of time.

One might wonder why animal spirits are so important to the shamanic practitioner since, unlike the shaman, many practitioners no longer live in rural village communities in close proximity to animal life. We no longer share our daily lives with animals that live freely in the natural environment. Why should the shamanic practitioner who lives in an urban and technologized world prefer an animal for a helping spirit rather than a human or angelic spirit? Certainly there are other non-animal spirits that assist the shaman in spiritual and healing work, such as the elementals, devas, angels, land spirits, and ancestral spirits and the more recently deceased.

Historically shamanism developed in tribal cultures where animals played a crucial role in human life and survival. Even though modern civilization appears to have transcended humanity's reliance upon animals to a great extent and the amount of wild nature continues to shrink year by year, we have not totally isolated ourselves from the Earth and the realms of animal life. Animals continue to haunt our dreams, imaginations, and fantasies. Young children, for example, dream more about animals than about family and friends, and not just domestic cats and dogs, but barnyard animals and wild animals, creatures they encounter primarily in zoos, books, television, and movies. It is almost as if in our first years, we are still programmed from earlier eras to have a rapport with and interest in wild animals.

American civilization itself is not far removed from animal life. A mere century ago, people in the largest cities allowed pigs to roam freely to consume garbage; transportation was horse-drawn; birds of prey routinely appeared in urban parks; and it was not unusual for a wolf, fox, or deer to wander into residential neighborhoods. Live chickens could be bought at neighborhood markets. Many people continued to visit grandparents and cousins who still lived on outlying farms in the countryside. Life—wild life—flowed more freely between urban and rural environments.

It is curious that the development of the modern zoo coincides with the gradual removal of animals from daily life, beginning around the turn of the last century. The popularity of household pets is a recent phenomenon also. A century ago cats were kept primarily to keep the mouse population down; and a barking dog protected homes from intruders. The notion of an apartment dweller living on the tenth floor of a high-rise building having cats or dogs is a relatively strange idea in human history. Yet today we have become a nation of pet owners. Clearly it seems some inborn need for contact with animals survives even though we live in a manmade environment in which the physical presence of live animals seems irrelevant.

ANIMALS: TEACHERS AND PROVIDERS

Throughout history animals have played important roles both physically and psychically, providing material support and spiritual insight for human life. Almost all the world's creation stories agree that animals have been on the planet longer than we have and therefore have a first-come, first-born status in our eyes. They know the Earth intimately from long association with it. They have secret lives, hidden deep in the forests, waters, mountains, and deserts where men and women seldom, if ever, venture.

Animals live naturally and spontaneously, doing what they are created to do without the self-doubt, uncertainty, complaining, and guilt that characterize human activity. They stand before us as paragons of creation, living as they were meant to live and surviving, sometimes cooperatively, sometimes competitively, with other creatures in a web of mutual dependence. Animals never lose their sense of themselves as spirit, responding with a fullness of spirit to whatever life presents to them, be it food, playful fun, sex, or death.

Our ancestors depended on animals for much of their material life. Animals provided food, clothing, ornamentation, tools, weapons, medicine, shelter, transportation, and companionship. They acted as harbingers of seasonal change, danger, and fluctuations in the weather.

Compared to human beings, animals collectively possess greater strengths and powers. In the animal population we find individuals who can run faster; swim better; see, hear, and smell more acutely; climb rocks and trees faster; hunt more successfully; and of course, fly. I doubt that even with years of practice, I would be able to get my pouncing skills on a par with my cat's. Many animals live longer and are physically stronger than we are. Some animals survive in environments too harsh and inhospitable for human beings, such as deserts, the bottoms of lakes and oceans, and in chambers bored deep into the Earth.

It is no wonder that ancient people saw animals as deities, or forms of deity, possessing wisdom, knowledge, and an intuitive relationship with other life that humans have to struggle hard to acquire, if we can acquire it at all. It is not surprising that our ancestors looked to animal spirits as teachers, companions, and guides through the mysteries of life. The ancient stories about human beings and animals sharing wisdom and knowledge before the Fall attest to the value of having animals as companions and teachers. The continuing folk and fairy tales about friendly animal companions on the hero's journey constitute a vestige of this older shamanic knowledge about our dependence upon animals. On some level, we sense that animals are exempt from many of the changes that took place when the Paradisal Age ended. Their calm self-assurance and continued practice of living according to the laws of nature, in balance and harmony with their environment, stand as a model for human beings, providing a standard for us, a reminder of natural laws, even as we who have the greater powers of creativity transform the environment.

POWER ANIMALS

The native peoples in the Pacific Northwest, such as the Coast Salish and Okanagon, speak of their helping animal spirits as power animals. This is not meant to imply that the spirit animal is physically large or strong. Power here means spiritual power that comes from inherent knowledge, information, or wisdom that the power animal willingly shares with its human companion. Every animal has power by virtue of its being part of nature and a necessary player in the game of creation. Whether it be Bear, Raven, Coyote, Mouse, Chipmunk, or Dolphin, the shaman believes that a particular animal spirit seeks out a particular individual to befriend because there is some mutual need between them, each being able to offer the other support and help in his or her journey through the many realms of existence.

Some people have had a strong affinity for a particular animal all their lives. Sometimes this totem animal may go back to a childhood toy or storybook that fueled a child's dreams and fantasies. As adults we may have preserved that interest in our childhood animal friends, collecting representations of them, reading about them, enjoying movies about them, and so forth. It comes as a disappointment to many people, but this animal may or may not be your power animal for shamanic practice. The horse, crow, or owl that always captured our imaginations as children and adults may not appear in one's shamanic work. I know this from my own experience, having been fascinated by whales since childhood. I may have been one of the few students in my high school class who read *Moby Dick* to the bitter end. I even continued to read it every few years, inspired by whale-watch outings on Cape Cod in the summers. Like so many people, I collected my favorite animal: paintings, woodcarvings, sculptures, calendars, note paper, t-shirts, and small figurines of whales made out of everything from glass to rubber. A rubber whale still sits on top of my computer monitor.

I was sure that a whale—or Whale, as it would be known as a power animal—would be my spirit companion when I began shamanic work. But I never met Whale on journeys for four or five years of shamanic practice. Only later did Whale appear as a helping spirit for a certain type of healing journey.

This is not to say that your favorite animal or family animal totem will not be your power animal. It merely means that you must begin your practice with an open mind and heart and allow the spirits to decide which power animal is most appropriate for you at this time. There is also a worldwide belief that the spirits, including animal and nature spirits, need us as companions also. The animal that becomes your first power animal may seek you out because its own spiritual needs or tasks are compatible with yours.

Be confident that your power animal and you are destined to work together for both individual and mutual goals, as well as the more universal goal of re-creating the paradisal condition in which humans and animals understood their mutual kinship. You might even think of an animal spirit companion as a prerequisite for shamanic journeying, because in order to enter the spiritual cosmos of nonordinary reality, you must first re-establish the kind of relationship with animals—or at least with one animal—that was intended at the very beginning: a relationship of mutual respect, support, and friendship.

Having an animal companion with whom you can communicate is the first step in re-entering that "time outside of time"—the First Time, Dreamtime, or Creation Time that still exists in the nonordinary realms beyond our normal state of consciousness. With an animal companion, you will not lose your way through the dreamlike realms of spirit, for animals have never lost their way through the realms of nature and the mysteries of the Earth. In a manner more direct and spontaneous than ours, animals leap up to life's many calls, confident that as both body and spirit, they know what nature requires, and what can be done and needs to be done to maintain their connections with the greater universe.

MEETING YOUR POWER ANIMAL

There are several ways that traditional shamans discover their power animals, all of which might be used by practitioners of core shamanism.

VISION QUESTING FOR A POWER ANIMAL

The most elaborate method for meeting an animal spirit is the vision quest or night vigil in a remote wilderness setting far from your home and usual environment. Traditions differ on the details concerning how many days and nights to spend, whether to fast or abstain from certain foods or drink, whether to remain awake the entire time or sleep when necessary, whether to be naked except for a blanket, and so forth. Practitioners of core shamanism can reflect on and evaluate the various methods that have been used around the world and select those that appeal to us and our circumstances. (Further instructions for vision quests are given in Chapter Six.)

The core idea is to spend at least twenty-four hours—although a longer period would be preferable—isolated, alone, freed from the normal distractions of life while praying to the spirits to reveal your personal helping spirit in the form of an animal.

If your power animal belongs to a species that lives in the region where you are questing, it might appear to you physically while you are on the vigil or quest. It's possible you will see several animals during your vigil; if so, you must send out a heartfelt prayer to each one as it appears, asking if its spirit is to be your power animal. If it is, it will make some obvious move or sound, some unusual behavior, which you will clearly know is an affirmative answer. It might, for example, reappear several times, or hang around even after it notices you, apparently unafraid of your presence; it might call out directly to you, or wake you in the night. You might not see any animals physically but dream of one while asleep. This is a reason you might not want to stay awake the entire time: an animal spirit may use a dream to appear to you.

On the other hand, depriving yourself of sleep for a couple of nights will create an altered state of consciousness in which you will be more aware of your surroundings both physically and spiritually. With your senses heightened, you might hear an animal deep in the woods or see a bird flying high in the sky that you would not ordinarily have noticed.

Fasting also quickens the senses. After abstaining from food for two or three days, one perceives colors as more vivid, light and shadow more distinct, sounds clearer. In this state of consciousness you may be more receptive to meeting an animal spirit—or put another way, an animal spirit may be able to get you to notice it more easily as a conscious, responsive, communicative being.

The shaman's prayer is a petition for help, acknowledging our weaknesses, and a call to higher spirits for strength, insight, wisdom, and power. Native Americans pray that the spirits take pity on us.

Fasting and staying awake are time-honored adjuncts to prayer, for they demonstrate our sincerity in asking for visions or spiritual help. As brief, self-imposed periods of suffering, they shine out into the universe like beacons, announcing our intention and sincerity; and the higher powers take notice.

Black Elk, an Oglala holy man, explained to Joseph Epes Brown in *The Sacred Pipe* that "crying for a vision" should be done in the spirit of "lamenting." "In the old days we all—men and women—lamented all the time." Some, like Crazy Horse, lamented "many times a year, and even in the winter when it is very cold and difficult." We should keep Black Elk's instruction in mind not only during our quest for a power animal but in all our journeying and visionary work. He says, "The most important reason for 'lamenting' is that it helps us to realize our oneness with all things, to know that all things are our relatives." [1]

A word of warning: Do not undertake a vision quest without knowing your strengths and limitations and without informing someone of your plans. In other words, do not fast for four or five days if you have never done so before. Do not go off into the wilderness alone for several days without someone knowing your whereabouts. Even in tribal cultures, an elder shaman knew the whereabouts of the younger person on the first vision quest.

DREAMING FOR A POWER ANIMAL

An alternative method for meeting a power animal is to ask your power animal to reveal itself to you in a dream at night. Since we live in a culture that does not value dreaming or encourage us to remember dreams, this is not always easy to do. In fact, you may have to try it for several nights or even several weeks, asking each evening before you go to bed for your power animal to come to you in a dream and make it clear that it is indeed your power animal. But take heart that you are not dreaming alone: if the power animal wants to use the dream to reveal itself to you, it will be part of your dreaming. The dream will be clear and vivid, and you will wake knowing you have made contact with a spirit helper in the form of an animal.

RATTLING OR DRUMMING FOR A POWER ANIMAL

Our early ancestors developed a variety of percussion instruments to use in sacred ceremonies: drums, rattles, click sticks, hollow logs, and clapping stones. They used these sacred sounds to communicate their deepest and highest aspirations to the spirits, including the spirits of nature, the forest, and the animal life that surrounded them on a daily basis. So the animals know that we humans use these sounds for sacred purposes. If we drum or rattle with the intention of calling the animal spirits to join us, they will. They will hear and hearken to the ancient sound.

Here is a procedure for meeting a power animal this way.

1. Darken the room, light a fire or candle, burn incense or sweet-smelling herbs, sit down on the floor, relax, and begin to rattle or drum in a steady, persistent, mesmerizing beat. Keep your eyes closed or slightly parted as you gaze at the candle or fire.

2. Let your mind and heart be open and receptive to images and sounds of animals. You might simply allow animals to pass through your consciousness, letting individual ones appear and disappear in a stream of images.

3. After a while, perhaps five to ten minutes, one animal will seem to be persistent in catching your attention; it may appear to hang around longer, or return again and again. You may begin to feel like you cannot stop thinking about this particular animal. It may seem like the animal or its energy is present in the room. This may be an indication that it is your power animal. Ask it if it is, and see how it responds. It should give you some clear sign, such as an affirmative movement or call, or perhaps it will speak, either in silent words that you hear in your heart or by an instantaneous thought transmission.

4. When you discover your power animal, continue drumming or rattling, holding its image in your mind's eye, allowing its presence to be near you. Feel its power. You might also rise up and begin to dance with it.

DANCING FOR A POWER ANIMAL

Dancing in itself is a way of meeting a power animal. Here is a method inspired by Michael Harner's instructions in *The Way of the Shaman.*[2]

1. Begin by rattling strongly and rapidly as you face each of the four directions, calling the animal spirits that dwell in each direction. Begin in the east, then turn to the south, west, and north, rattling about a minute in each direction. My personal practice is to call birds and winged creatures from the east; fur-bearing animals with paws and claws from the south; fish, whales, dolphins, and other water creatures from the west; and horned, antlered, hoofed animals or animals that run in herds from the north.

2. After you have completed the four directions, raise your rattle overhead and acknowledge the spirits of the sky and the heavenly realms above the sky. Then bend low and shake the rattle near the Earth, honoring the spirits of vegetation and fertility.

3. Continue rattling with your eyes closed or partly closed, and begin to dance. Try not to become self-conscious even though these movements may seem strange to you. No one is watching except the spirits who will not be judgmental, knowing that this is not performance dancing or partner dancing. There are no right or wrong movements, steps, beats, or patterns. Basically what you are attempting to do is to allow the spirit of the animal to move your body.

4. Begin at first by simply swaying in place or walking in a slow circle around your fire or candle. Call the animal spirits to join you and ask the animal that is your helping spirit to move your

body. Eventually you will sense the presence of a particular animal near you or even within you. Your body will move as if on its own; you will not have to think about dancing. Your animal spirit is dancing through you.

5. It doesn't matter whether you end up simply walking around in circles or you begin to dance quickly and dramatically, imitating the movements of the animal itself, either in a realistic fashion or in a stylized version of that movement. What is important is that the animal spirit move your body. Continue dancing, acknowledging the animal's presence until you feel a solid connection with it. When you feel it is time to stop, do so and welcome the animal into your life, asking it to leave some of its spirit or energy in your body.

These last two methods for meeting your power animal—rattling or drumming and dancing—can be greatly enhanced if you ask a partner or two to join you. The additional sounds of drumming and rattling will facilitate your entering the altered state of consciousness in which you will be more receptive to seeing and hearing the spirits. If your partners have power animals of their own, they will call them to be present also, and these animal powers will summon yet others, one of which will be yours.

JOURNEYING FOR A POWER ANIMAL

This will probably be your first journey. Use the method described in the next chapter for journeying, and when you proceed down the tunnel or passageway into the Otherworld, send out a heartfelt call to the animal spirit that is your personal helper and guide to meet you on this journey. Here are some guidelines for this journey.

1. If an animal is waiting for you when you emerge from the tunnel, ask it if it is your power animal and to give you a clear sign,

such as nodding, frisking with you, or running off and reappearing to you in different ways. Acknowledge it, and spend the journey time getting to know it. Ask it to show you its skills, powers, or what it likes to do.

2. If no animal is waiting, you may have to look around a few moments, call for it, announce your presence. Sometimes the spirits test us to see how sincere we are. They may play coy for a while before they show up.

3. It's also possible that you will see several friendly animals waiting for you. If so, you will have to ask the one that is your power animal to make itself known by some distinct sign. It will.

WHAT TO DO IF NO ANIMAL SPIRITS SHOW UP

If you rattle, drum, dance, or journey and find no animal spirit approaching you to be a power animal, try again later. Keep in mind that your power animal may be testing you to see how determined you are to meet it. Shamans would say that you do have a power animal, that everyone has helpful, guardian spirits in the animal kingdom, or we would not have survived beyond childhood. It is similar to the belief that we each have a guardian spirit in the angelic realms, whether or not we acknowledge it, call it by name, and regularly communicate with it. So finding a power animal is not so much a question of searching as it is of making yourself open and receptive so that the power animal you have had for many years can make itself known to you.

HAVING SOMEONE RETRIEVE A POWER ANIMAL FOR YOU

Another way to find a power animal is to ask a friend who practices shamanism to journey for the express purpose of retrieving a power animal for you. The procedure for this is explained in the Chapter Nine.

DEEPENING YOUR RELATIONSHIP WITH YOUR POWER ANIMAL

Shamanic practice depends on strong, personal, ongoing relationships with helping spirits. The power animal is often a shaman's primary spirit helper. For most practitioners of core shamanism, the power animal is the guiding spirit that accompanies us on every journey, our major link with nonordinary reality. It can also be a source of information and other kinds of help, but first and foremost it is a guide through the Otherworld. It knows the geography of nonordinary reality and can take us where we need to go for specific information or experiences, such as to other helping spirits, both animal and human, who will become additional teachers in the spirit world.

I am sometimes asked in doing soul retrievals how I know where to go in the spirit world to find lost souls. (A soul retrieval requires a journey to restore power to a person who has suffered soul loss due to intense trauma or suffering that caused part of the person's soul or life force to leave the body.) Quite frankly, I don't know where lost souls hang out. But I have a special power animal who does, and she takes me there and introduces me to the specific soul parts to bring back for a client. Although it seems odd to say it, soul retrievals are not all that glamorous. I feel rather like a carrier for a sort of spiritual Federal Express, delivering the goods as promised. It is really my power animal who knows where to take me and how to bring me and the lost soul back to this reality.

Power animals function something like a combination of companion, tour guide, spiritual advisor, and psychic chum. Your success as a shamanic practitioner depends on the depth and richness of your relationship with your helping spirits, a trusting relationship which, like relationships in ordinary reality, cannot be developed overnight. Months or years of practice may pass before you get to know your power animal (and other spirit instructors) well enough to know what they can and cannot do. Over time you will most likely acquire other power animals as well, each with a specialty area or a type of knowledge that it shares with you.

Like any good friend, your power animal will expect certain considerations and commitments from you, and here are some suggestions.

- Don't ignore your power animal and only seek it out when you need to journey.

- Make an invocation or say a "good morning" prayer to it each day.

- Put up a picture of your power animal where you will see it each day.

- Wear a charm or pendant in its honor.

- Make acknowledging your power animal part of your body practice by calling it to join you when you run, walk, ride a bike, or swim.

- Let your art practice include drawing, painting, sculpting, or writing about your power animal.

- Ask your power animal in what way it would like you to acknowledge it or spend time with it on a daily basis. You can always negotiate if it asks something that is really impossible or unrealistic, like getting up at three in the morning to dance with it. (Spirits don't have the same need for sleep we do!) Make a counter-offer, compromise, but come up with some activity, ritual, or practice that can be done on a daily or almost daily basis in order to be aware of your power animal and begin to develop a strong, ongoing relationship with it.

REVEALING THE IDENTITY OF YOUR POWER ANIMAL

In some native cultures shamans do not reveal the identities of their power animals to others for fear that hostile shamans might use this knowledge to undermine their power and authority. Or if they do reveal their power animals, it is only to selected individuals whom they trust explicitly. Most shamanic practitioners today do not live in cultures where enemy shamans or magic-workers threaten their well-being. Nevertheless, it is wise not to speak openly or carelessly about your power animal. Holding the identity of your power animal as a trust or special secret is a way to honor your relationship with it. On the other hand, there are times when it is appropriate, maybe even necessary, to reveal its identity, such as in teaching or doing healing work with someone. The best approach is to ask your power animal directly under what circumstances you can speak openly about it or in what circumstances never to speak about it, and then honor its wishes. Certainly it would seem wrong to speak of it in a boastful or bragging manner for no other reason than to impress others with your shamanic skills. You would not want to make the subject of your power animal the chitchat of cocktail parties, or boast to other practitioners that your power animal can beat up their power animals. Even if your power animal could eat someone else's power animal, this is not a subject for one-upmanship.

WAYS YOUR POWER ANIMAL MIGHT DEEPEN ITS RELATIONSHIP WITH YOU

As mentioned above, a relationship with a power animal is a two-way street. You may discover that your power animal is appearing to you in various ways so that you will not forget about it. Following are some common ways in which you may discover your power animal popping up in ordinary life.

• You may begin to see your power animal in ordinary reality more frequently after learning what it is. If the animal is common in your geographic area, such as a crow, fox, raccoon, deer, or hawk, you may encounter it outdoors.

• If the animal does not live physically nearby, you may begin to see it in magazines, on billboards, on television, or in the movies.

- You may hear people talking about it in conversations.

- You may begin to dream about it.

A psychological (and skeptical) explanation for these appearances is that once you have some special interest in a particular animal, you are naturally more conscious of its image so you will seem to see it around more often. A shamanic view, however, is that the animal is truly appearing in some form or other, using ordinary objects and situations in your life to call your attention to it because, like you, it wants to develop a relationship for shamanic work. The web of animal and human spirits is vast and surprising, stretching across time and many places of encounters. You may even have some truly startling encounters with it or the power animals of people you know and work with.

One time I did a soul retrieval for a young man who practices shamanism, in exchange for cutting up some firewood for me. For two nights he came over after work with his chainsaw and cut up some dead tree trunks and branches from the woods around my house. Then he returned for the soul retrieval. The very next night a lame red fox appeared on my front porch. My two cats announced his presence by some unusual meowing, louder than normal but in no way menacing. I looked out the door and the two cats and the red fox were sitting on the porch within about five feet of each other. None of them seemed upset by the others' presence. (Even the cat who prides herself on her pounce technique wisely decided this was not prey.) I went out and the fox looked at me for a few moments, then got up, trotted right past me down the front steps, and disappeared into the woods. For the next few weeks the fox hung around, getting along with the cats very well. Then just as suddenly, it disappeared and never returned.

About that time, I called the young man for whom I did the soul retrieval to see how he was doing. We talked about the soul retrieval and then chatted a bit about what was going on in our lives. I told him about the red fox. He informed me that the red fox is one of his power animals.

As I think back on this, I am sure the red fox was a messenger from the young man's own spirit world. I also think that his working around the area cutting wood with the intention of using the work as barter for spiritual work imprinted his own spirit on the place and made it more receptive to his own animal spirits. The fox's lameness may even have been a manifestation of the man's injured soul for which we were doing healing work.

In any event, synchronicities such as this are powerful reminders to us that the universe knows and cares about what we do. Our practice has ramifications not only in our interior lives but in our external lives. The two worlds are really not separate; they continually overlap, allowing us to move from one reality into another. We just need to be alert for the occasions when the two realities break in on each other. And when we aren't alert, then perhaps our cats will call us to take notice.

If you are new to shamanic practice or have not been practicing regularly, use the methods suggested in this chapter to discover your power animal and deepen your relationship with it. Ask others who have more experience than you for advice and help, so that you and your power animal become a strong team. When you feel ready, learn the technique for the shamanic journey described in the next chapter.

CHAPTER THREE

THE SHAMANIC JOURNEY

A shaman is an explorer of doorways—doorways from ordinary reality into nonordinary reality, portals leading from the physical world into the spirit world. In Celtic spirituality these are considered "thin places" where the two worlds are in closer contact with each other, where the spirit world flows into the physical world, where spirits and mortals can pass with relative ease. Also known as "power spots," these places are found all over the world, some secret and personal, others world-famous, such as Stonehenge in England, the Black Hills in South Dakota, the Skellig Islands off the Irish coast, the Serpent Mound in southern Ohio. In the history of the human spirit ordinary people, whether ancient or modern, are lured to places where they perceive a greater power, energy, or spiritual force. And when we have felt the transformative and invigorating presence of the invisible powers, we long to experience them again and again, to be back in those realms where eternity meets the temporal world, where we know that there is more to the universe than we can perceive with our physical senses.

In seventeenth-century Scotland, a young boy known as the "Faery Boy of Leith" took his drum each Thursday night (a night considered auspicious to the Celts) into the hills outside Edinburgh. The historical account reports that men and women from the nearby towns joined him to "pass through invisible doorways" into the faery landscapes where they feasted, danced, drank, and sang, then flew to far-off lands for more adventures before returning to Scotland and ordinary reality. The Scottish journeyers returned to their homes in the city and waited until the following Thursday, when they reconvened. It seems life was far from dull or dour in Scotland on Thursday nights! Modern shamanic practitioners, as well as tribal shamans from other cultures and centuries, would recognize in this practice the classic shamanic journey into the spirit world.

What makes a shaman different from other mystics and visionaries is the *intentional* journey—or soul flight—into the spirit world. In other words, unlike the common perception that mortals must wait for spirits of nature or the dead to make contact—an occurrence that happens more frequently than most people realize—the shaman *initiates* contact by going directly into the spirits' world. Rather than waiting for the spirits to visit us, the shaman becomes the visitor into their invisible realms. Because they know the entry points, shamans can cross the borders of ordinary and nonordinary reality at will, enter the spirits' reality, and develop the skills, understanding, and competence for functioning in that dreamlike world.

ENTRIES INTO THE LOWER WORLD

A shaman sends her or his spirit (or consciousness) through a personal entrance into the Otherworld, and in so doing intentionally begins the shamanic journey. So the first step in becoming a journeyer is to locate your own entry and learn the procedure—the formula, if you will—for beginning a journey.

Entries into the Otherworld are of two types: portals that "open into the earth" for lower-world journeys and portals that "lead to the other side of the sky" for upper-world journeys. We will look at lower-world entries first.

The Siberian shaman Sereptie entered the Otherworld by descending the roots of a tree. At one point in his initiation a male spirit who sprang out of the roots told him, "You must come down through the root if you wish to see me." Later Sereptie was told that a hole that appeared in the ground was the one through which "the shaman receives the spirit of his voice." Sereptie recalls that "the hole became larger and larger. We descended through it and arrived at a river with two streams flowing in opposite directions." Yakut shamans in Asia speak of this type of entry in the Earth as "the Hole of Spirits."[1]

A spring or well is a natural entry into the spirit world in many cultures. In Europe these were often guarded by a female spirit or goddess who in Christian times was transformed into a female saint or the Virgin Mary. The notion of gifts of power or healing from the Woman of the Sacred Waters is found in many contexts. Arthur received the sword Excalibur from the Lady of the Lake; many of the thousands of pilgrims who journey to Lourdes in France are healed by waters dedicated to the Virgin Mary.

The !Kung shaman K"xau from the Kalahari area in Africa reported, "I dance. I enter the Earth. I go in at a place like a place where people drink water. I travel in a long way, very far. When I emerge…I am climbing threads…I follow the thread of the wells…."[2]

During his initiatory illness, an Avam Samoyed shaman of Asia was carried first into the middle of the sea, from which he emerged and climbed to the top of a mountain. There a spirit who was the Lady of the Water nursed him to health; her husband the Lord of the Underworld gave the shaman an ermine and a mouse to be his animal guides on lower-world journeys.[3]

These experiences of entering the Earth, finding animal guides, and learning the geography of nonordinary reality are at the heart of core shamanic practices.

FINDING YOUR ENTRY

To begin, select an opening into the earth that you know about in ordinary reality. It might be a cave, a crack between two boulders, a well or spring, a hollow tree that leads down through the root system, a waterfall that veils an invisible entry in the rocks behind it. Here are some characteristics that might apply to your entry.

- The opening can be a place you saw only once in your life or a place that you regularly see or visit.

- It can be a place from your childhood or early life or some contemporary spot.

- It can be smaller than you because your physical body is not going to go through it, only your consciousness or spirit.

- Most important, it should be a place that holds some particular fascination for you—a "thin place" where you intuitively sense spiritual power or earth energies.

- If you know of no such opening in ordinary reality, you can imagine one, but an entry that truly exists in the physical world is preferable because it clearly reinforces your experience of passing from one type of reality into another. It allows you to begin in this physical, everyday reality and leave it to pass into a nonphysical, dreamlike reality.

DISCOVERING THE TUNNEL TO THE LOWER WORLD

Immediately within the opening or on the other side of the opening, make yourself see a dimly lit tunnel, corridor, passageway, hallway, or chute that descends downward, either sharply or gently. The tunnel may be only a few feet long or it might seem as long as a city block, leading straight ahead or bending. When you are in sight of the tunnel's end, you can see—or make yourself see—a brighter, well-lit area just beyond. That is the edge of the Otherworld.

Bear in mind that this opening and tunnel are not a passageway into the *ground*. You are not journeying into the dirt or soil, only to discover rocks, bugs, slime, roots, and other unpleasant surroundings that you might associate with a hole in the ground. Instead you are journeying *into a magical realm that you perceive as existing just beneath the surface of ordinary reality*—in this case, the surface of the Earth. For this reason you must see the tunnel immediately upon passing through the entryway. If it is not there or your rational mind tells you that you should be seeing dirt and bugs, *create* a tunnel. It's acceptable to imaginatively fashion the beginning features of the shamanic journey. This is just another way of saying that you consciously and intentionally control the time and place the journey begins.

You begin the journey in the "imaginal realm" where you can, if you choose, create images that provide the shapes and forms that allow the spirits to communicate with us. Aristotle said that image is the language of the soul. Do not hesitate to help your soul begin its journey into the spirit world. Although you are consciously creating the initial images of your journey, you will soon see that the journey takes on a life of its own and the spirits come of their own free will—you are not making it up.

EXPLORING YOUR ENTRY AND TUNNEL

Become very familiar with your entry and tunnel before you begin your first journey. Familiarity with the entry and tunnel impresses the reality of this place on your consciousness. When you emerge at the other end of the tunnel, your consciousness will have shifted into a nonordinary state, into the imaginal realm where you can experience places, animals, and things that exist outside your ordinary state of consciousness. So it is important that you create for yourself a clear experience of moving from one type of reality into another, or put another way, of moving your consciousness from an ordinary state into a dreamlike state.

Follow these steps to become familiar with the entry and tunnel:

1. Sit quietly, close your eyes, take a few deep breaths, and in your mind's eye, see the entry as it exists in ordinary reality.

2. Look around for a few seconds, allowing the place to affect each of your senses. Notice colors, shapes, flora and fauna, the sky, the soil, weather conditions, the air, scents, and sounds.

3. Next imagine yourself passing through the entry and standing in the tunnel. Again engage your senses, noticing the texture or shape of walls and floor, their color, the atmosphere, the light at the end of the tunnel and its color. Do not proceed down the tunnel, but stand there for a moment looking around.

4. Then imagine yourself backing up or turning around and returning through the opening in the Earth back to the place where you began.

You should practice seeing or sensing these places now before reading further.

THE SHAMANIC STATE OF CONSCIOUSNESS

If you are not a visualizer, you may wonder if you can journey. You can. I know many excellent shamanic practitioners who claim they very seldom, if at all, "see" things on their journeys. But they sense them; they intuitively "know" what is there, where they are, what they are doing. Some report that they see colors or atmospheric shapes and textures, but nothing distinct, and yet they too "know" that within these sensations they are with their power animals and spirit teachers. So although we tend to use the words *see, visualize,* and *image* for the sake of convenience, keep in mind that in terms of your own experience, the sensations may be nonvisual.

Some people hear their journeys rather than see them. They hear the voices of spirits, or they "hear" the gist of what their spirits tell them, almost like instantaneous thought transmission.

As you reflect upon the experience of scanning down your tunnel to get familiar with it, you will probably be aware of several things. You will certainly be aware that you *made* yourself do this. You may even have the sensation that you *made it up*. This is all right because "making the journey begin" means making yourself see or sense things that lead from ordinary reality into nonordinary reality. *You are making it happen.* There is a difference between making it happen and making it up. You will come to understand this distinction better as you practice.

For example, you are making up (that is, creating) the formula that you use to initiate journeys: a place in nature, an entry into the Earth, the tunnel, the light at the end. You make yourself see these things. You are creating the shapes of these things, which are the images the spirits use for communicating with us (along with the images and shapes they produce on their own). But you are not making everything up. The difference should be obvious when you reflect on this exercise. Even though you made yourself see the entry and pass through it, and maybe even programmed yourself to see a tunnel, you did not have to consciously decide the shape of the tunnel (whether rounded or straight walls) or the texture of the walls (whether ribbed, smooth, rough, plated, or something else). You may not have decided consciously the length of the tunnel—you looked for the light at its end, and there it was at a certain distance. You may have had the same experience in noting the color of the light at the end; you automatically and spontaneously saw or sensed that it was golden, white, blue, reddish, or whatever.

This is an important phenomenon to consider: the shamanic journey, like this beginning scenario, is *a combination of intentional and nonintentional experiences and sensations.* You can make things happen without making everything up. The shamanic journey is different in this way from a guided meditation or what are called "pathworkings," in which you are instructed what to see and do.

The most common question people ask when they are learning to journey is whether they are "just making it up" or "is it really happening?" as if there must be a contradiction between the two. There need be no contradiction. Because you are in control of the journey (we will consider this more fully a bit later), you can make things happen; your intention determines much that occurs on the journey. But because you have entered another reality, the spirit world, you are not totally in control and cannot determine everything that occurs. The spirits are autonomous; the nonordinary places and events of the shamanic journey exist in a dimension where we are only visitors, not rulers.

In many ways this differs little from our experiences in ordinary reality. We can determine many things—what we wear, where we will go, what we will order to eat, how we will spend an evening. But we do not determine all the details: you run into a friend you didn't expect to see; the menu now includes some interesting dishes it didn't have last month; the quiet evening at home is interrupted by phone calls; your VCR taped the wrong program. We should expect the same on the shamanic journey: a combination of "planned" and "unplanned" activity.

Some journeys, even for experienced shamanic practitioners, may seem to be more spontaneous than others that seem "forced" or "made up" or a result of wishful thinking. Each practitioner learns to discern the subtle differences in these experiences. It may seem that a journey is 80 percent spontaneous and 20 percent made up, but this is not necessarily more effective or meaningful than one in which these percentages are reversed. The more spontaneous journeys may seem more satisfying because they are more convincing as authentic journeys beyond our selves, our egos, and our narrow perceptions. But a journey that seems forced or a product of wishful thinking can still provide the relevant information, instruction, healing, or experience for which we intended to journey.

I recall a divination journey I did for a woman concerning a decision she was trying to make about her career. I felt the journey was not very "authentic" because I was tired that night and the spirits did not seem particularly cooperative, or it might have been that my conscious mind and ego were too active and fretful during the journey. In any event, I felt as if I were "making it up." But when the drumbeat changed to bring me back, I suddenly passed through a strange landscape that had an enormous giant holding a globe on his back. Atlas! I thought, curious about why he was there since this had nothing to do with the previous part of the journey. However, I didn't question this apparition; I just returned with my power animal to the tunnel and came back up.

I related the journey to the woman, hoping it would prove to be relevant information for her problem, but somewhat skeptical because the journey seemed forced. To my surprise I could tell that much of the journey did make sense and held some meaning for her because she kept nodding her head affirmatively as I related what occurred. But when I told her that for a brief moment I saw Atlas holding the world on his shoulders just as I was returning, her eyes lit up, and she exclaimed, "That's it!" It reminded her of the statue of Atlas in New York City's Rockefeller Center which, unbeknownst to me, was important in her decision because one of her job opportunities was located there. Atlas was a key to understanding the entire journey and a key to her decision.

So be prepared for your first journey or your thousandth journey to "feel" less spontaneous than you wish. On the other hand, your first or thousandth journey may be the most spontaneous you will ever have. The point here is simply that because we are walking in two worlds at once, we can never predict which world—that is, which state of consciousness—will dominate. But fortunately the spirits can work with us in any state of consciousness, so they can give us the relevant information or instruction regardless of how we feel about the authenticity of any given journey.

YOUR FIRST SHAMANIC JOURNEY TO THE LOWER WORLD

When you have practiced seeing your entry and tunnel and are familiar with them, you are ready to do a journey. You will need someone to drum for you, or you may use a drumming tape. Decide how long you want to journey; about eight to ten minutes is sufficient for the first journey. Your drumming partner should have a clock in view so that he or she can change the drumbeat and call you back when the time is up. (Drumming instructions are explained in the next section of this chapter.)

The procedure for journeying is quite simple.

1. Lie on the floor on your back (with a pillow beneath your knees or under your head if you need it). Place a bandanna or scarf over your eyes to deepen the darkness behind your eyelids. Try to be as relaxed or limp as possible. Take a few deep breaths and see the location in nature where your entry is.

2. When the drumming begins, look around this place of entry for a few moments as you previously practiced, engaging your senses, noticing colors, shapes, sights, sounds. Then go through the entry and make yourself see the tunnel if it is not spontaneously there, and proceed down it toward the lighted area at the end.

3. When you emerge, you will be in a landscape of some sort. Look around. Call your power animal to join you and ask it to show you around this area just inside the Otherworld. (We will talk about things to do on this first journey a bit later.)

4. When the time is up, the drummer will change the beat. Some segment of your ordinary consciousness—perhaps 10 percent or maybe only 1 percent—stays in ordinary reality. This is the part that always knows subliminally that you are lying on the floor listening to a drumbeat. This part of your awareness will hear the change in drumming. At that point, tell your power animal that it is time to return.

5. Your power animal will take you back to the tunnel so that you can proceed upward and emerge through the original opening.

6. Spend a few moments reorienting yourself before you open your eyes.

Power animals have various methods for bringing you back to the tunnel. Here are the three most common methods.

- On some journeys your power animal might lead you back by retracing your path step by step through all the terrains you explored.

- Your power animal might simply point to the end of the tunnel wherever you are, saying something like, "There it is," even though it may seem that you have traveled a great distance away from it. This is possible because nonordinary reality, like a dream-place, is a shapeshifting world outside of time and space as we think of them.

- Power animals can run or fly with you very quickly through a foggy or misty landscape and, within seconds, be back at the original point where you entered the Otherworld.

When you return to the tunnel, thank your power animal for the journey, say you will be back, and then go up the tunnel.

THE DRUMMING TECHNIQUE

Through his extensive work with experiential shamanism, Michael Harner has discovered and perfected a drumming technique that works well for most people. In his book *The Way of the Shaman*, Harner explains the typical drumbeat for shamanic practice and the effects it has on states of consciousness.[4] In brief, a continuous and monotonous drumbeat of about 205 to 220 beats per minute is suggested. Do not vary the beat in timing or intensity. This is not music but a mesmerizing sonic driving intended to create an altered state of consciousness. Do not expect that the drumbeat will put you into a deep, coma-like trance.

The word *trance* is a bit misleading, since we generally take it to mean a complete blanking out of ordinary reality and a rather helpless state of inactivity during which we experience visions or voices over which we have no control. This is not the shamanic state of conscious-ness nor is it conducive for the shamanic journey. As mentioned above, a certain percentage of your ordinary awareness remains somewhat attentive to what is occurring in the physical environment. You may hear someone in the room sneeze or a siren go by outside. This does not mean you are not in the shamanic state of consciousness needed for the journey. Simply ignore the distraction and pull your awareness back to what is occurring on the journey in nonordinary reality.

If one is drumming, the method for alerting the journeyer that the time is up and he or she should return to ordinary reality, is as follows, based on Harner's work.

1. The drummer stops the continuous, steady beat, and pauses for a second.

2. The drummer gives four strong drum rolls of seven beats each.

3. Then the drummer beats as rapidly as possible for thirty to forty-five seconds.

4. Finally, the drummer beats four more drum rolls of seven beats each, somewhat slower and softer than the usual drumbeat.

This callback procedure gives you about a two-minute warning that it is time to end the journey and return. During that time, ask your power animal to return you to the tunnel as described above, thank it, ascend to your initial departure point, and come back into ordinary reality.

WHAT TO DO ON THE FIRST JOURNEY

On the first journey you should aim primarily at exploring the Otherworld, learning what it feels like to function in another reality. It will probably seem like a waking dream, or perhaps a lucid dream, in that there will be a magical sense that time and space do not exist and the rules of ordinary reality do not apply. Explore the landscape just on the other end of the tunnel. Get to know it well. This is the area you will tend to emerge into on subsequent journeys.

You should use these early journeys to become acquainted with your power animal since it will be a constant companion on future journeys. You can ask it to show you:

- its powers and abilities, letting you experience them and share in them to whatever extent it allows at this time;

- its favorite places and power spots in the Otherworld; or

- places of power or rejuvenation that will be important for you to know as well.

JOURNEY TO THE UPPER WORLD

In the cosmology of traditional shamanic societies there is a threefold division of the universe: upper, middle, and lower worlds. This triune structure may be built into the human psyche because it corresponds well to the way we perceive space as bipedal creatures walking upright and living on the surface of the Earth. For people who perceive unseen realities beyond the physical world, it makes sense that there should be a reality beneath the Earth, another above the sky, and a third right here, albeit invisible, in the middle where we live. In some cultures shamans journey primarily to the upper realms; in others they journey primarily into the lower worlds. (There is also a middle-world journey, which we will look at in Chapter Five.)

Most people in our culture have already been introduced to the notion of upper and lower worlds through the popular versions of *Alice in Wonderland*, a lower-world journey, and the Hollywood movie *The Wizard of Oz*, an upper-world journey. Shamans from any indigenous culture around the world would have no problem relating to these stories; in fact, they would probably have personal accounts not very different from Alice's and Dorothy's.

Just as the lower world is at the end of a tunnel beneath the surface of the earth, the upper world is at the end of a path or route that leads through a hole in the sky. The notion of an opening or hole in the sky is common in indigenous societies. The Pole Star has often been considered an entry through the sky. Yakut shamans think of the stars in general as holes in the "great tent" of the sky; the Milky Way is the tent's seam. Carlos Castaneda calls the twilight the "crack between the worlds." [5] The red light on the horizon at sunset could be used as an entry to the other side of the sky. There are other openings as well, not visible to the naked eye: "thin places" in the texture of the sky, in the bowl of the heavens, in the cosmic skin that stretches across our universe—openings your power animal knows about and can lead you to.

To reach these openings you will need an ascent, a route that connects ordinary physical reality to the realities above the sky. This might be a slanting ray of sunlight, which native people in New York's Hudson River Valley call a "wampanac." It might be a rainbow, which many cultures, including the Norse tribes of ancient Europe, have considered a bridge between the worlds. The experience in *The Wizard of Oz* of going "over the rainbow" into a magical land is consistent with shamanic thinking. In tribal cultures the typical dwelling had a fireplace in the middle of the floor and a smoke-hole built into the ceiling directly over it. In this setting shamans journeyed up the smoke, through the smoke-hole, and into the sky. Climbing a magical tree, stalk, or vine that continues up and through the sky is another method (the folktale "Jack and the Beanstalk" taps into this technique). In Australia shamans climb a cord that goes up into the sky. Carib shamans in Guyana dance on ropes and swing in the air until a spirit appears and invites them: "Come to the sky on Grandfather Vulture's ladder. It is not far." Then they climb a spiral ladder of sorts. [6] The Hindu rope trick in which the fakir climbs a rope and disappears at the top seems to have its origins in early shamanic practices.

The important point here is to begin, as you did for lower-world journeys, with some natural phenomenon, such as smoke, a sunbeam, rainbow, tree, vine, or sunset, that can be used as a pathway into the sky, a route your consciousness or spirit can travel up. Choose one that appeals to you and decide on the place in ordinary reality where you will find it: a woodland clearing, a hilltop, a yard or park, a fireplace.

The physical route you choose corresponds to the opening and tunnel into the Earth for a lower-world journey. The opening at the end of the tunnel corresponds to the slit or hole in the sky through which you will enter the upper world. Just as the lower-world journey was not into the actual ground, the upper-world journey is not into outer space. Outer space is still in the middle world; it is part of ordinary physical reality. Instead you are journeying *into the magical realm on the other side of the sky*. On your first journey you may spontaneously come to this opening and pop through it, or you may have to make yourself see it as you ascend into the sky, just as you may have had to consciously make the tunnel end so that you could spring out into the lower world. Remember that you are *supposed to imagine* this beginning formula to initiate the journey.

When or where do you meet your power animal on an upper-world journey? You can ask your power animal to join you on the Earth before you begin the ascent if you wish, or to catch up with you during the ascent, or to meet you after you pass through the opening in the sky. When the drumbeat calls you back, ask your power animal to lead you to the opening in the sky, pass through it, and return down the path you ascended, be it smoke, tree, rainbow, or wampanac.

As on the first lower-world journeys, use the upper-world journeys to explore the landscape, find out what's up there, and have your power animal introduce you to a celestial spirit teacher or instructor.

It's a good idea to spend the first four or five journeys exploring both the upper and lower worlds. Familiarity with the immediate terrain on the other side of your entries will allow you to have more control over beginning journeys. This area is also a place to meet power animals and other spirit instructors, and it is the setting for many types of journeys. Later your power animal can show you more distant regions in the Otherworld—places you might need to go for other types of journeys, either for yourself or for others.

SUMMARY: LOWER- AND UPPER-WORLD JOURNEYS

Before we continue, here is a checklist of the basic steps in both lower- and upper-world journeys.

LOWER-WORLD JOURNEY:

1. Lie on the floor; cover your eyes with a bandanna.

2. Repeat the intention or purpose of your journey to yourself three times.

3. Drummer begins to drum.

4. See your entry into the lower world; look around for a few seconds, engaging all the senses.

5. Go through the entry and down the tunnel; emerge into the lower world.

6. Call your power animal to join you (if it has not spontaneously joined you at the entry, in the tunnel, or at the other end of the tunnel).

7. Tell your power animal the purpose of the journey.

8. Let your power animal conduct you through the experiences that will satisfy the purpose or intention of the journey.

9. When the drumbeat changes to the callback beat (or when the purpose of the journey is achieved), ask your power animal to take you back to the tunnel.

10. Come up the tunnel; come back out the entry; look around; slowly let this scene fade as you become aware of your physical surroundings.

UPPER-WORLD JOURNEY:

1. Lie on the floor; cover your eyes with a bandanna.

2. Repeat the intention or purpose of your journey to yourself three times.

3. Drummer begins to drum.

4. See the place in nature where you will begin and your means of ascent (smoke, tree, rainbow, sunbeam, etc.); look around for a few seconds, engaging all your senses.

5. Go up the ascent; pass through the opening in the sky; emerge into the upper world.

6. Call your power animal to join you (if it has not spontaneously joined you on the ground, on the ascent, or on the other side of the opening).

7. Tell your power animal the purpose of the journey.

8. Let your power animal conduct you through the experiences that will satisfy the purpose or intention of the journey.

9. When the drumbeat changes to the callback beat (or when the purpose of the journey is achieved), ask your power animal to take you back to the opening in the sky.

10. Come down the ascent; return to the place in nature on the ground; look around; slowly let this scene fade as you become aware of your physical surroundings.

WILL YOU GET LOST IN THE OTHERWORLD?

There are legends about people going into the spirit world and not returning. European folklore is filled with tales of ordinary people slipping into the faery realms, not to return for seven years or more—or ever. In tribal cultures there are stories of shamans who take the final journey at the end of their lives, allowing their souls to enter the next world and leave this plane forever. Should we worry about not being able to get back? No. Most of the stories about people trapped in the spirit world are about individuals who are not experienced with these kinds of realities, people who do not know the basic shamanic methods of journeying and returning safely that you have learned in this chapter. The point of journeying with spirit companions, either in animal or human form, is that they know the territory, they know where to lead you for spiritual growth and life-affirming experiences. They would not take us into realms that are harmful or from which we cannot return. Our personal helping spirit companions have only our best spiritual interests at heart.

But you may discover that you do not *want* to return. The overwhelming reports from people who practice shamanism are that many journeys are so satisfying, enriching, comforting, and blissful that journeyers wish they could go on forever. But the drum calls them back, and the 10 percent or so of their ordinary consciousness knows that the time is up for this particular journey. It is time to leave what the Celtic people call the "Land of Beauty, Youth, and Promise," where the faery music is too heavenly to describe. Time to leave the Otherworld that the Kashia Pomo shaman Essie Parrish described as a road with "flowers and flowers and flowers out of this world." [7] Time to leave the spirit realms where, according to Black Elk, the people "were happy and had plenty...(had) fat and plenty horses, and singing hunters were returning with their meat." [8]

A Chuckchee shaman said that on the shamanic journey, "I rose above the limits of the world...my feet were walking on the far side of heaven." [9] Many philosophers and mystics from Plato to contemporary shamans have said that our True Home and the True Earth are not this physical landscape where we live our ordinary lives, but the Otherworld that we encounter only in myth, dream, and mystical experiences like the shamanic journey. It seems obvious that we would not wish to return.

If the Otherworld is such a satisfying realm, why then do many shamans relate encounters with monsters and demons, describing life-threatening experiences they claim are dangerous and terrifying? Do "the far side of heaven" and the "Land of Youth and Beauty" have their shadow regions as well? In the next chapter we will look at the kinds of light and dark experiences that confront the shamanic journeyer, just as they have confronted spiritual seekers throughout the ages. We will learn what the dark journeys are all about and how they contribute to our spiritual practice.

 Chapter Four

SACRED HORIZONS

A spiritual path begins wherever you are at the moment and leads outward. In our spiritual practice, based on the shamanic journey, we start in ordinary reality and enter the nonordinary realms of mystery and wisdom that surround us. In this chapter we'll look at the "sacred horizons" that encompass our lives and form the edges of time and space in both physical and spiritual ways. We'll discover how to give the physical world a sacred dimension by consecrating the four directions, the four basic elements of earth, air, fire, and water, and the seasons of life so that they become reflections of the greater spiritual cosmos in which we live.

HORIZONS OF POWER AND BLESSING

Horizons fire the imagination and fuel our sense of wonder, leading us out into the vaster regions of the universe. From mountain or hilltop, in the trackless desert, on desolate tundra or the flat, endless plains, from a boat or island in the middle of the sea, the human eye gazes outward to the edge—and beyond. In that crack between the worlds where sky and earth meet, we sense the doorway to infinite possibilities. Here the guiding lights of the vaulted heavens—sun, moon, stars, and planets—rise up over the eastern edge of earth and sea, cross the sky, and disappear below the western horizon for eternal renewal.

The horizon joining earth and sky, however, is but one of many circles that encompass our lives. We live in ever-expanding circles and spheres of relationships, with countless radii leading us outward to search, work, play, and explore. When we sit in a circle around a fire, the light shines outward past each of us to the edge of darkness in fields and forest. Like firelight, horizons stretch out to our left and right, before and behind, and even above and below our gaze, for the sense of mystery and adventure that resides beyond the flat horizon of the Earth is also present in the upper world overhead and the lower world underfoot. The horizon beckons and promises long life, for although it seems to set limitations and boundaries, it continually advances ahead of us, opening up newer regions to explore, further mysteries to encounter, and higher levels of consciousness with which to understand the powers that fill the universe.

The Navajo Emergence Myth contains a blessing for such an explorer who would journey to the edge of the world:

Then go on as one who has long life,
Go with blessing before you,
Go with blessing behind you,
Go with blessing below you,
Go with blessing above you,
Go with blessing around you,
Go with blessing in your speech,
Go with happiness and long life,
Go mysteriously.[1]

Other Navajo refrains, constructed with this same format, speak of "Beauty" before, behind, above, below, and surrounding the singer.

In the house of long life, there I wander,
In the house of happiness, there I wander.
Beauty before me, with it I wander.

Beauty behind me, with it I wander.
Beauty below me, with it I wander.
Beauty above me, with it I wander.
Beauty all around me, with it I wander.
In old age traveling, with it I wander.
I am on the beautiful trail, with it I wander.[2]

The Navajo term *hozho*, usually translated into English as "beauty,"
is much richer in meaning. It is the beauty that signifies balance, harmony, order, and the well-being that comes from being in tune with the
laws of nature. It is within this all-encompassing "Beauty" that the
Navajo hopes to walk, wander, live, grow old, and eventually die.

In the Highlands and islands of Scotland where the older Earth-centered spirituality and its shamanistic elements survive, we find similarly
structured prayers. Here the Celtic supplicant calls upon the Creator with
the terms "Being of Strength," "Source of All Life," "Creator of the
Elements," "The Three of Life," the "Sacred Three," the "Secret Ones,"
and simply the "Powers." In remote rural regions where life is lived in
close contact with nature, animistic reverence for the divine power within nature characterizes the spiritual lives of the Highlanders and
Islanders, much as it did for their Celtic ancestors of pre-Christian times
who found the numinous in nature. Here nature and the divine presence
(which is inseparable from nature) surround every activity. The encircling
prayer of the Navajo echoes in Celtic refrains.

The Three Who are over me,
The Three Who are below me,
The Three Who are above me here,
The Three Who are above me yonder,
The Three Who are in the earth,
The Three Who are in the air,
The Three Who are in heaven,
The Three Who are in the great pouring sea.[3]

Saint Patrick himself wrote one of the original "breastplate" prayers, given this name because they summon powers and sources of protection to wrap themselves around the speaker like a breastplate of armor.

Christ in me, Christ beneath me, Christ above me,
Christ on my right, Christ on my left,
Christ when I lie down, Christ when I sit down,
Christ when I arise,
Christ in the heart of every one who thinks of me,
Christ in the mouth of every one who speaks of me,
Christ in every eye that sees me,
Christ in every ear that hears me.[4]

The abiding sense that spiritual power surrounds us, either in the form of Beauty, Christ, a Trinity of Divine Powers—or Nature herself—is intrinsic to the shaman's vision. As practitioners of shamanism, we must look for the signs and omens in nature that reveal this pervading power and strength.

THE FOUR DIRECTIONS

Shamanic practitioners follow a spiritual path that leads the soul through nature to the divine. Wherever we go, we are always and inevitably in the center surrounded by power, but paradoxically we are not meant to *stay* in the center. From the center of spiritual horizons, we venture forth, searching for personal growth in each of the four directions.

Each person's unique journey through life passes through cyclic points and seasons, analogous to the points on the horizon and the seasons of the year. In cultures where the effects of the seasons on nature are viewed as the work of divine beings or spirits, the turning of the year becomes a sacred event in which human beings can and should participate, for in the annual seasons we find the rhythms and patterns of our own interior life. The four directions and four seasons form a holistic web in which divinity manifests and cuts across each individual's life at many points. Meditate on the four directions along the lines suggested below.

THE EAST

It begins with the rising sun. The sky lightens, and the dawn announces a new day. The sun is reborn and grows strong in its rising. As in the early days of spring, the earth is fresh, and the human heart responds with hope, the promise of renewal, and the chance of living a day better than those that preceded this one.

THE SOUTH

As the sun climbs higher in the sky, it swings through the south, giving the earth maximum light at midday. Human activity is at its fullest, like the fullness of summer when bright, warm days call us forth for work, play, and adventure in the vast outdoors.

THE WEST

When day is done, the setting sun draws our attention westward, the direction of completion, fulfillment, and death. As the day itself dies, our thoughts turn homeward where we rest and recall the day's activities, and prepare the memories that will accompany us into the next stages of life.

THE NORTH

North is the place of shadows, the quarter of the sky where the sun never travels in its daily course. Here it is cold and dark, the realm of midnight, of sleep, dreams, visions, and eventual regeneration, as the Earth and the human spirit wait to be reborn into a new dawn.

Every twenty-four-hour cycle we relive this pattern of eternal renewal, as each circuit of the sun around the horizon encompasses the fullness of human life. From our vantage point at the center, we can see ringed around us the creative forces that ebb and flow through nature, year by year, season by season, day by day by night. The creative force encircles and empowers us, for we too are part of the created world, filled with the Creator's spirit. Our own creativity shares in the creativity of the cosmos that keeps the seasons turning, the sun rising, the Earth renewing itself.

The shaman is attuned to the reciprocity of rhythms and finds in them sources of spiritual power. A shaman's personal life is ringed with spirit helpers, surrounding him or her with energy, knowledge, beauty, grace. As a spiritual path, shamanism can enlighten the stages of human growth and development through which we must progress, like the sun on its daily journey, so that we advance in the right direction, en route to our True Home in the next life.

MEETING THE ALLIES IN THE FOUR DIRECTIONS

Begin a series of journeys to the four directions shortly after making your first exploratory journeys into nonordinary reality. These journeys expand the sacred geography in which you practice and give you spiritual references for the physical environment where you live. Here are guidelines that you can adapt to your own practice.

1. Ask your power animal to take you into the four directions to introduce you to your helping spirit in each direction. Spirit helpers may appear in animal or human forms. You can make this four separate journeys, one for each direction.

2. On meeting each spirit, learn its name or what it wants to be called.

3. Ask it to tell you what particular mysteries that direction holds for you and what kind of power or spiritual assistance you can gain from that direction.

4. Specifically, ask each spirit what gift of power or knowledge it has for you. One way to word this request is to ask: "What virtue

or strength can I develop by drawing on the spiritual power of this direction?"

5. Make repeated journeys to these spirit teachers, develop a relationship with them, and learn how they can help you become strong in the virtues they offer.

By "virtues" I mean the old-fashioned ones, such as honesty, compassion, service, loyalty, patience, tolerance, understanding, and so forth. These traditional virtues are great mysteries. They are meant to be unraveled, explored, adapted, studied, practiced. You may need to be initiated into them, so this would be additional information to get from the spirits. Ask them to help you develop a plan of study or practice, a concrete course to acquire the art or skill of practicing the virtues and making them permanent fixtures in your life. Living these virtues on a daily basis requires spiritual strength and courage because we live in a culture that does not place great value on them. Many people pay them lip service but consider it naive to try to live by these virtues in modern society.

Once you have discovered what gifts are available to you and what virtues are required, you must commit yourself to practicing them, no matter how hard it is to do so. We hear many accounts of tribal shamans who suffered great sorrow, depression, even physical illness, for refusing the call to be shamans. Shamanic practitioners meet similar sufferings by refusing to accept the obligations that shamanic knowledge brings. Often these obligations center on the practice of virtues that run counter to the prevailing values in modern society.

As shamanic practitioners, however, we live in more than just modern, urban society. We are "walkers between the worlds," ever seeking to realize the oneness and unity of those worlds. The old-fashioned virtues still exist in the Dreamtime or Original Time that we explore on shamanic journeys. The power that comes from our helping spirits is the power to practice those ancient virtues and live those original values.

In fairy tales we hear that the "old ways" existed "once upon a time," but as shamanic practitioners we learn from our power animals and spirit advisors that no time is ever "once," for all time and times exist in the present.

HONORING THE SPIRITS OF THE FOUR DIRECTIONS

Compose a daily prayer or ritual that acknowledges the spirits in the directions where they reside. This prayer/ritual can be the breastplate invocation structured like the Navajo and Celtic prayers that literally wrap power or beauty above, below, in front, in back, and on the left and right. The prayer can be worded very simply. Here are two examples. Substitute the name of your spirit ally for the ones given here.

> I honor the East, Spirit of Swan, power of honesty.
> I honor the South, Spirit of Cougar, power of service.
> I honor the West, Spirit of Michael, power of courage.
> I honor the North, Spirit of Deer, power of compassion.

Or,
> I see Swan flying in the East, she is looking at me,
> I pray to her for honesty,
> I see Cougar running in the South, he is looking at me,
> I ask to be of service,
> I see Michael standing in the West, he is looking at me,
> I ask for courage,
> I see Deer, watching in the North, he is looking at me,
> I ask for compassion.

When saying these prayers, face each direction and shake a rattle for a few moments to announce your intention to the spirits in that direction before you make the invocation. Be mindful of these spirit helpers as you go through your day, being equally aware of the four directions. At work, home, school, or wherever you spend time, note the directions, particularly where the sun rises and sets. Let these orientations become so much a part of you that you are never "lost," so to speak, but always mindful of yourself at the hub of spiritual power and knowledgeable about what kind of power and help comes from the spirit ally in that direction.

MEETING THE ADVERSARIES IN THE FOUR DIRECTIONS

Among the reasons for following a spiritual practice is the hope of becoming a more enlightened human being who realizes and embodies the noblest qualities of human life. If we follow the Buddhists' insights on this, however, we must practice without becoming too attached to the *goal* of enlightenment, allowing it to occur, if it will, as a kind of spiritual spin-off of our daily practices. This attitude is not always easy to maintain, but we can learn from the lives of shamans and mystics who concentrate primarily on their daily practice, not the ultimate goal of enlightenment.

Nevertheless, spiritual growth requires us to confront our shadow or darker natures. Every person is a combination of light and dark qualities—what traditionally are called virtues and vices. Many students of human nature tell us that it is not possible to totally eliminate the shadow side, that such a goal is meaningless, for it denies the basic truth about human existence that everything contains its opposite. Still, it is reasonable to hope that negative traits can be tempered and tamed. In fact, human decency requires it, not to mention that human society would become unbearable and inevitably unlivable if we did not strive to mitigate the darker sides of our personalities with the brighter virtues and aspirations. As a spiritual practice, shamanism offers us a method for working with the shadow or adversary.

In classic shamanic literature the adversary often appears as a monster or demon, threatening the very life of the shaman. Some shamans speak of battling the demons, even destroying them. Others elude their adversaries or outwit them. These are the sources for shamans' reports that the Otherworld has "evil spirits" intent on harming or destroying us. Considered from the perspective of spiritual development, these encounters may be viewed as struggles with those forces that challenge our commitment to pursue the mystical life, that test our resolve to unite our own creativity with the greater creative forces of the universe. The "evil spirits" are destructive because they are the antithesis of creation; and yet in some mysterious way, as many religions teach, the destructive powers are part of creation. Things must die to be born; life and death walk side by side; destruction and creation are partners in a great dance.

In theological terms, the demons try to prevent our union with the Divine Spirit or our realization of that union. Demons are enemies in the sense that they test our courage and endurance, casting doubt upon our ability to live in the fullness of creation. They lead us to despair, lure us into the "dark night of the soul." They tempt us to retreat into what the Huichol shaman Matsuwa calls our "little lives." He warns people not to be "caught up in their own little lives" to such an extent that they fail to get "their love up to the sun, out to the ocean, and into the earth." He teaches that "sending out your love in the five directions—the north, the south, the east, the west, and the center—brings life force into you." [5] In Matsuwa's instructions we hear echoes of the Navajo song and the Celtic prayers acknowledging the "life force" that dwells in all directions and wraps us with power and protection.

Part of our practice should be to get our love out from the center, especially to reach the "demons" that block our spiritual growth, that hope to confine our love, prevent us from sending it out into the greater universe, out to the source of our life. They scare us into huddling in the safety of the center and try to convince us we cannot survive on the edge of the horizon, that it is too risky to get our love out, up, and into the Greater Universe.

Here is a program of journeys to meet the adversaries of the four directions and get your love out.

1. Ask your power animal to take you on four separate journeys into each direction.

2. In each direction, ask the ally of that direction to tell you about the adversary that awaits you there.

3. On this journey, or the next one if you wish to prepare for it first, ask your power animal and ally to introduce you to that adversary.

4. When the adversary appears to you, ask it what gifts or powers it can offer to accompany those of the ally's. It is a common experience for people pursuing the spiritual life to discover that demons and monsters are really allies in disguise, or put another way, they can *become* allies if they are confronted and befriended.

5. When the adversary appears to you in ordinary reality, rather than trying to elude or destroy it (or worse, give into its demands), challenge it, and ask it to reveal itself as a positive force.

Adversaries, monsters, and demons can and do transform themselves for several reasons.

First, shapeshifting is a common occurrence in nonordinary reality. Second, everything contains its opposite, so what looks monstrous or threatening has a cooperative, beneficial aspect as well. Third, the particular power of any spirit is a form of energy, and as energy, it can be used for good or ill.

Once befriended, the baneful influence of a spirit dissipates and the spirit's energy can be directed to some positive goal. For example, you may discover that one of your adversaries is the Spirit of Anger, which as a vice in ordinary reality may wreak havoc in your life by souring your own experiences and frightening people who are important to you. Powerful emotional forces like anger and resentment exist in ordinary reality but have their spiritual components in nonordinary reality as well. Or put another way, you, the Angry One, also exist in nonordinary reality in spirit form. You might consider the angry monster you meet to be a spiritual being that is part of you, yet can separate from you, appearing as a "lower" form of yourself who seeks to subdue your "higher" self. In this way you can view your spiritual struggles in terms similar to the shaman's battles with evil spirits.

Let's say on a journey into nonordinary reality you encounter the Spirit of Anger, hoping it will teach you how to channel your anger into legitimate circumstances where this emotion is justified and appropriate, where it might benefit you or society. You must be prepared, however, to have a fierce conflict with your adversary in both ordinary and nonordinary reality, similar to the battles described by traditional shamans haunted by demons and monsters in both the physical and spiritual realms.

One journey may not turn the demon into an ally once and for all. It may still plague you in daily life, reappearing in situations where you lose control and erupt just as before. But have courage and be confident that you do not struggle with the demon alone. You have power animals and spirit allies in all directions. You have strength in front, behind, above, below, on the right, and on the left. You are encompassed by spiritual power. The test of wills is just that, a test to prove that you will not be intimidated into giving up and retreating into the confines of your little ego-world. When you have demonstrated your commitment, you can ask the monster to change into a permanent ally, and it will.

EARTH, AIR, FIRE, AND WATER

The sacred horizon is the home of the four elements as well as the four directions. Since ancient times people have associated the four elements with the four directions and four seasons of the year. The most common associations in the Northern Hemisphere are as follows:

- Air is associated with the East and Spring, for it is the eastern sky that first brightens in the earliest light of dawn. Then the air is fresh, as in spring, when warm, moist breezes herald the rebirth of nature.

• Fire is associated with the South and Summer, for southward lie the warmer zones and the steamy equator itself. Life is lived outdoors more extensively in the southern regions, as it is in summer when the long hot days make us intensely aware of the sun's fire.

• Water belongs in the West and with Autumn, for water runs downward into the earth, like the setting sun. Water seeks its resting point, as the sun seeks its evening rest below the horizon, as human beings, exhausted from the day, seek a place to lie down and rest at day's end.

• Earth is associated with the North and Winter, for these are dark, dense, and in their own ways, impenetrable. Earth casts a shadow, and as the sun swings through the South each day, shadows swing across the North. In winter occur the longest nights of the year.

The shaman knows and works with the four elements and the spirits of the seasons as much as with animals and plants. Not only as healing properties but as spiritual instructors, the elements and seasons can teach us about the sacred mysteries. We are encompassed by the four elements and we are composed of the four elements, for the Creator decided that we should be made of the same stuff as the rest of Creation. We are mostly water, and with the same salt content as the great oceans of the Earth. Our lungs take in oxygen, which is carried through the blood to every cell of the body, without which those cells would die. Our internal fire is 98.6 degrees Fahrenheit, and if it varies even slightly, we feel weak. Our physical bodies are composed of minerals, bone, and trace elements that are found in the Earth, not to mention the saline quality of our bodily fluids, which is the salt of the Earth.

Greek philosophers were obsessed with discovering which of the four elements was the "original stuff" of the universe, of which everything else is made. Heraclitus thought it was fire; Thales suggested water; Anaximenes opted for air; while Xenophanes voted for earth. In the fifth century B.C. Empedocles wisely called attention to the fact that the known universe was actually composed of all four. Since then workers of magic, healers, alchemists, psychics, and spiritualists have fiddled with each of these individually and in various combinations to understand the mysteries and secrets of the cosmos. The shaman too has not been immune from wondering in journeys through nonordinary realities how the spirits of these four elements can assist us in understanding personal power and what the four have to teach about their—and our—Creator.

TALISMANS, POWER OBJECTS, AND OTHER "POWERPHERNALIA"

When airport security reached an all-time high, I resorted to casting spells of invisibility over my drum and power objects when passing through the gates where they frisked me for weapons. I decided on this after a sweaty incident in the Detroit airport.

I had placed my drum bag on the conveyor belt and watched it pass into the x-ray machine that was commanded by a sour, no-nonsense agent who peered intensely through the glasses perched on the tip of her nose, which twitched as if smelling something unpleasant. She held my bag in the viewer for what seemed like an awfully long time, squinting her eyes into ever narrower slits. Finally she barked, "Sir, is this your bag?" Everyone in the area listened up. I identified it as mine, and she demanded, "What is *in* here?" I said, "Two drums."

With a flick of her head, the agent summoned another guard, who unzipped the bag so slowly I could almost hear each tooth on the zipper disengage. People in line behind me were starting to stack up and breathe impatiently. Carefully the two inspectors lifted the flap and looked in. When the woman nodded her head to give the all-clear, the other agent reached in gingerly, fumbled around for a few moments, looked up at her, and said, "Two drums." He re-zipped the bag; she slid it over to me and said with a somewhat plastic smile, "Have a nice flight." That was the moment I decided to use shamanic skills to get through security.

Shamans can become invisible or shapeshift into other forms that will hide their true identities. Saint Patrick once turned his men into deer so that enemy ambushers would not notice them passing by. Now as I approach the airport security stations, I ask my power animals to make my drums, rattles, stones, feathers, and other power objects invisible or to look harmless, especially the plastic baggy of sage, cedar, and lavender that I burn as incense but that looks suspiciously like marijuana.

As you practice shamanism, you will inevitably acquire paraphernalia which, once in a drumming circle that was turning giddy, we decided should be renamed "powerphernalia." Why do we need sacred stuff?

As the encompassing prayers teach us, we are encircled by power— the sacred power of divinity, which has had various local names over the centuries and across the continents. Embedded in the four elements, this life force surrounds us whether we ask for it or not, because the elements are all around us, as well as within us. Even though we think of our souls as immaterial and capable of transcending any physical form, they cannot escape the elements themselves while we live within this physical creation.

As a spiritual practice we can consciously keep the power of the four elements around us and with us ritually in the form of talismans and power objects. Native shamans carry pouches, magic bags, and other types of satchels and bundles that contain their sacred tools. In Native American circles, these pouches are called "medicine bundles," because the word *medicine* refers to that sacred power the native healers use in their work. Often as we look at these traditions from outside their cultures, the sacred objects kept hidden in the bag take on a strong and strangely mysterious aura. We suppose them to contain magical and spiritual powers beyond imagining. And indeed, the manner in which truly powerful spiritual healers use their medicine objects indicates that there is some numinous significance connected to those objects.

And yet how disappointed Westerners can be to discover that sacred bundles often contain "nothing more" than old bones, some stones, a feather or two, perhaps a seashell. Anthropologists used to explain the ordinariness of these objects in terms of the shaman's quackery or self-delusion. The shaman, they said, was a fake who tricked clients and followers into thinking such ordinary objects contained great spiritual and healing power; or shamans were deluding themselves, bolstering their sense of self-importance by keeping mundane objects secret and calling them magical. And yet the objects worked! Or to put it more accurately, they worked *for the shaman* because the shaman's power depends on receiving help from sources beyond himself or herself, and these simple objects represent those sources of healing power.

Even what appear to be old sticks and stones can serve as conduits of healing energy. The object, regardless of whatever power it contains in itself, becomes a source of fascination for the shaman that builds up the shaman's belief and trust in the spirit of that object to influence ordinary events. The shaman is not a quack in spite of the traditional theatrics and vaudeville quality that shamans might incorporate into a healing ceremony for the sake of entertaining onlookers and creating the sense of excitement that something important is happening. The shaman knows that certain tools and objects are sacred because he or she has developed relationships with the spirits of those objects, who have taught the shaman the secrets of power.

As part of your shamanic practice, collect a few basic objects that represent the four elements and use them to deepen your relationships with the spirits of those elements. This is not to say you must wear a "medicine bundle" in the Native American sense, but rather in some way carry and revere the sacred elements that serve as mnemonics for remembering your power and its source in nature and the spirits of nature.

You can ask your personal helping spirits for instructions on what specifically to collect, but some of the more common objects used for the four elements include the following:

AIR

A feather can represent air because as part of a bird's wing it flew through the air. Incense or herbs create sweet-smelling fragrances when burned that are often used in ceremonial work to represent the spirit of air, and when a feather is used to waft the smoke around the room for purification or blessing, the feather takes on the scent and carries it afterwards. So the feather can have both associations with air: its natural connection of having been part of a bird's wing and the ceremonial importance that you give it by using it with sacred herbs or incense.

FIRE

Fire is not easy to carry around with us, but there are natural objects that can contain the spirit of fire:

- A crystal can represent fire because it catches the fire of the sun and gleams brightly when turned.

- Wooden objects that are seared or woodburned carry the imprint of fire.

- Candle wax used in ceremonial work can be dripped into water, where it congeals to a small pebble-like shape. Since the wax once contained the heat of the flame, it can stand in for the spirit of the flame.

WATER

A seashell or a pebble from a creek or beach holds the mysteries of water within it. Alternately, a small vial or bottle can be filled with water from a sacred spring or the ocean and carried.

EARTH

Earth is the easiest element to keep with us since the options are endless: stones, dried leaves, soil, pebbles, crystals, small branches, pieces of wood, clay, ceramic, or even animal bone.

If you are inclined to carry these objects in a bag or bundle and are concerned about appropriating practices from contemporary native people for whom the medicine bundle tradition is still vital, you might consider the Celtic crane-bag as a European version of this. In Celtic lore there is a mysterious bag made from the skin of a crane that originally belonged to the God of the Sea, filled with his sacred objects, including a shirt, a knife, a hook, swine's bones, a helmet, and shears. The crane-bag pops up in later stories concerning other Irish heroes, such as Finn MacCool and Conaire. In every instance, by having the bag the owner receives knowledge of the bardic and druidic mysteries, which means visionary knowledge from the Otherworld. In fact, cranes are traditionally guardians of the Otherworld, scaring away unwelcome intruders. (Waterbirds in general are seen as Otherworldly creatures because of their ability to function in three worlds: in the air, on the water, and on land.) To possess the crane-bag and its sacred trove is to possess otherworldly knowledge.

Considering, then, the shaman's bag of sacred objects, we can draw on the crane-bag tradition from Ireland and Britain to inspire our own practice, assured that keeping objects representing the elements in a special bundle for visionary or ritual use is an ancient and widespread practice. In the spirit of core shamanism, we do not need a bag made from the skin of an actual crane because we are developing new and personal traditions for the modern world. The bag could be made of any material, although you might reflect on this and choose a material that has some significance for your own practice. Then design, construct, and decorate the bag as part of your art practice.

FAMILIES OF SPIRITS

When we consider the web of spiritual power that radiates outward from and inward to our center, we discover over time that each of us looks out toward a unique horizon populated with helping spirits who support and challenge us, either as allies or adversaries. As you create a spiritual cosmos within which to practice shamanism, you'll come to know the animals, plants, seasons, elements, deities, culture heroes, and other natural phenomena that comprise your sacred circle. You will have a vast web of spiritual help to draw upon. At first, you may not recognize the interconnections among these spirit helpers, but over time you may come to see them as a coherent family—or perhaps several families—of spirits.

In tribal cultures where families and clans were organized around a central totemic figure, each member of the group thought of himself or herself as related to the others through an intimate association with the totem, which might be a particular animal or plant. So, for example, the People of the Crow thought of themselves as being descendants of an original parent-figure who was Crow or the Spirit of Crow. The Crow became the emblem or symbol of both the group itself and its individual members. The group or clan name was often the name of the totem. In Europe the Celtic tribes had names like People of the Boar, Ravenfolk, or People of the Oak.

What is interesting for our shamanic practice is that often the totem spirit was an emblem for other animals, plants, and elements, not just a symbol for the human tribe. In other words, there were "tribes of spirits" who were considered to be people of the same totem. In Australia, for example, beings other than humans can belong to the same clan and have the same totem. Rain belongs to the Crow Clan and thus has something of the nature of the Crow in it. The Crow is the uniting and integrating principle for all the beings who belong to the same totemic group. When a person dies, the burial scaffold should be made of the wood from a tree that belongs to the person's totemic family. What this teaches us is that when native people such as the

Australian Aborigines look out into the natural world, they see many beings to which they are related because they belong to the same totem family and have the spirit of that totem within them. In this way native peoples discover a mystic kinship with certain plants, elements, and animals in nature.

As we consider the beings that sit on our personal horizons, comprising our mystic cosmos, we can ask them to show us how they are related to each other. It's possible they are all members of the same spirit family of which you are also a member. It may be that they fall into several separate groups, each with its own guiding spirit or principle. These are issues for you to discover through journeys and discussions with your spirit helpers about how they work in your life and what specific talents, skills, and knowledge they offer you. Knowing the interrelationships among helping spirits lets you meet them more frequently in ordinary reality. For example, if Bear is your power animal and you do not live in an area where there are bears, you will not see them. However, if you know that your Bear spirit belongs, let's say, to snow, winter, sunset, and maple trees, you will have Bear's kinfolk around you on a regular basis. In fact, Bear may be the totem for that group of beings, or maybe Bear is simply a member of the clan that encompasses these beings, and some other spirit or deity is their totem. You can find out by journeying specifically to ask your helping spirits to show you the interrelationships between them and you.

There is a mountain named Bull Hill I climb every Sunday morning as part of my shamanic practice. Over the months I have met the spirit of the mountain, who has a specific role to play in my shamanic training. When an elderly relative of mine passed away, her spirit began to accompany me on these weekly hikes, and I learned from my power animal that the mountain and my relative were in the same spirit family. I also discovered about a hundred feet off the trail a large boulder resembling a human skull. On later journeys the skull-boulder appeared to me as the spirit of the Severed Head, an important symbol in ancient Celtic spirituality and a concept that inspired what I call the Severed Head journey (see Chapter Nine). Other spirit beings have joined these over time, and I now understand the "mystic family" that they represent and how I am a member of it. They take their places on my sacred horizon, and when I pray to be encompassed, they draw close. When I climb Bull Hill on Sunday mornings, I am making a pilgrimage to their shrines.

THE SACRED HORIZON IN ART

The sacred horizon that develops around you through the course of your shamanic practice can become the material for your art practice. In some Native American traditions sacred shields depict the spirits and animal helpers important to the shield's maker and owner. Siberian shamans draw maps of the spirit world on the skins of their drums, usually in highly stylized representations. The heraldic imagery in Europe evolved from earlier representations of family spirit totems on shields and armor. In many cultures shamans honor their spirit allies by depicting them on their ritual garments, either in representational or nonrepresentational form. The Huichols weave symbols of the *neirika*, the threshold to the Otherworld, into beautiful yarn pictures. Similar artwork is painted onto hides. The Navajo create sand paintings, usually in circular forms, showing the directions and the spirits that encompass the world. The mandala, a form of sacred art from Tibet, also depicts horizons, directions, and various levels of consciousness that are part of the spirit world. It is appropriate to use your sacred horizon and the spirits that dwell on it as themes and material for shamanic art.

If you do not feel drawn to the graphic arts, try playing a small musical instrument such as a flute, harp, or dulcimer—something that can be played without much formal instruction. Flutes and simple stringed instruments lend themselves to this quite easily and can be carried with you outdoors. Take the instrument, bless it, call your helping spirits, and ask them to give you the music. At first you may feel awkward, but spirit-teachings have quick and profound effects. In no time you will be playing well. Then you can play to honor the spirits in each direction. Face each direction as you play for that direction and call the spirits with your music to create a sacred circle in which to work. Of course, you can study any instrument formally for your own satisfaction, but as a shamanic art practice, the idea is to let the spirits give you the notes and melodies.

THE SHAMANIC CALENDAR

As we become more aware of nonordinary reality in our daily lives, we seek to transform the ordinary into the numinous that corresponds to our experiences in the Otherworld. If we know the horizons and seasons that encompass us both here and beyond, we can also discover the calendar that reflects those seasons. Native people kept track of annual events by the phases of the moon, the revolving of stars and constellations across the night sky, and the position of the rising and setting sun on the horizon. Today we have replaced these natural markers with the paper calendar of twelve months.

Part of our shamanic practice can include creating a personal calendar of feasts and celebrations. We can draw on the old tribal and village calendar of Europe with its solstices, equinoxes, and cross-quarter days.

THE QUARTER DAYS

The summer solstice is around June 21.
The winter solstice is around December 21.
The autumn equinox is around September 21.
The spring equinox is around March 21.

THE CROSS-QUARTER DAYS

The feast of Imbolc on February 1 honors the first signs of spring.
The feast of Beltane on May 1 is the beginning of summer.
The feast of Lammas or Lughnasad on August 1 is the first harvest.
The feast of Samhain on October 31–November 1 is the beginning of winter.

There are many ancient and modern traditions associated with these eight days. As part of your academic practice, read up on these and discover which features correspond in some manner to the way you live or to where you live. Many books on European folk customs, witchcraft, neo-paganism, and anthropology will give you ideas on this. Create your own ways to celebrate and honor these turning points in the Wheel of the Year. Chapter Nine has suggestions for shamanic journeys at these times.

You might also develop a twelve-month or thirteen-moon calendar as a personal way of understanding the months of the year on the standard Gregorian calendar. In the spirit of native customs, consider what is happening in nature each month, or what personal activities characterize the seasons as you live your life. Work, play, vacations, school, and travel can suggest names for the months or moons. Our culture already does this to some extent: September is back-to-school month; June is the wedding month; July and August are vacation months; Thanksgiving through New Year's is the holiday season. Find your own references and names, and be aware of them in ways that reinforce your shamanic practice. The weather column in the daily paper will tell you the times when the sun and moon rise and set, and when the new and full moons occur. You can coordinate shamanic activities and rituals around these times.

My own moon calendar is based on where I live in the Hudson River Valley in New York State and on the activities that are currently part of my life. Its associations are as follows:

January: Moon of Staying Indoors
February: Moon of Waiting for Spring
March: Moon of the Returning Sun
April: Moon of Singing Dawns
May: Moon of Young Flowers
June: Moon of the Long Days
July: Moon of the Open Road

August: Moon of the First Harvest
September: Moon of Melancholy
October: Moon of Falling Leaves
November: Moon of Coming Home
December: Moon of the Long Nights
Thirteenth Moon: Moon of Mystery

THE CIRCLE AND CROSS

The circle that is crossed or quartered is supremely satisfying to the human imagination as psychic or mystical space and has been a mainstay of religious art since Paleolithic times. The circle itself represents an unbroken boundary or enclosure separating and protecting the realm within from the realms without. The four points of the cross indicate gateways through that boundary and pathways leading to the center, the point of perfect balance and wholeness. As sacred space, the encircled cross allows spiritual power to move in three directions: radiating from the center outward, ringing the circumference, and converging inward toward the middle. To be in the center is to be surrounded by "Beauty" in the Navajo terms of harmony and balance, or what the Celts call "the Three of Life," the "Sacred Three," "the Secret Ones," "the Powers."

The circle itself, with or without the cross, has long inspired the human imagination with a sense of wholeness, perfection, and completion, for every point on the circumference is equidistant from the center; there are no discernible beginnings or endings; and the whole is perfectly and smoothly balanced and accessible from the center. There are no hidden corners or abrupt turning points as in straight-edged and angled geometric figures. There is no place to lose your way.

From earliest times our ancestors have drawn, etched, and constructed circles, often squaring them with crosses or quarters. Circles of giant megaliths in western Europe, Native American medicine wheels, mandalas painted in Tibet, Navajo sand paintings, tall Celtic stone crosses, and Paleolithic rock art found in many parts of the world depicting crossed circles all bear witness to the worldwide fascination with this figure that is itself indelibly etched in the human mind.

For the Hopi the crossed circle is the symbol for life-in-balance. It is thought that among the prehistoric rock artists, this symbol stood for the sun, for it suggests the fiery center from which rays spread out in all directions, and in some forms it is painted with the flaring tangents of the swastika that make it appear to be rolling or spinning, as the sun rolls across the sky. In historic times the encircled cross is the astrological symbol for the planet Earth. All three associations are appropriate, clearly pointing to the perennial concern for balance and wholeness, for life arises and prevails only in the right balance of energies from the earth and the sun.

We stand at the center of this sacred circle wherever we are, and paradoxically, we are always seeking it. We look outward in all directions with the eye of the shaman, searching the locations, scanning for sources of personal power that reflect the Great Power that created the world at a moment we like to think of as the beginning of time.

But does time have a beginning?

Although we have been educated to believe in time and space as linear, we are not born at one end of a line, living and working our way along it, eventually reaching the other end. Not even death is an ending but, like the ancient Celts said, "the center of a long life." Everything wants to be round. The Oglala Sioux medicine man Black Elk said, "The Power of the World always works in circles, and everything tries to be round." He claimed that the "circle of the four quarters nourished" the Sacred Hoop of his people. "The east gave peace and light, the south gave warmth, the west gave rain, and the north with its cold and mighty wind gave strength and endurance." [6]

Our spiritual practice should remind us of the circularity of experience, the roundness of creation, and the curving, spiraling energies moving through us. Rather than finding our place in line, let's find our place in the center of a horizon filled with blessings surrounding us. If we find the sacred locations along that horizon, we can draw them inward to us, even as they call us outward. We will then truly appreciate the Web of Life, for we will be living it, discovering our True Home along every strand that radiates from the center, along every strand that encircles the center, and we will learn that the Web is endless and timeless.

⊚ CHAPTER FIVE

MIDDLE-WORLD JOURNEYS

We wake up in the morning to a certain cast of light in the sky, and a particular weather pattern sets the tone for the day ahead. By force of habit, we splash water on our faces or take a shower, eat breakfast, and drink a cup of coffee. Outdoors the sun shines on us; we get wet from the rain; a refreshing breeze carries with it a sweet fragrance. In the course of the day we walk over soil, concrete, sand, grass. A favorite landscape catches our eye. Birds twitter in the setting sun, and we are suddenly aware that night is falling, and the day is over.

Encounters with the elements are the stuff of everyday life, and allowing for minor adjustments due to modern living, these are the same encounters men and women have been having with the elements since the dawn of human history. And yet our relationship to the natural elements is dramatically different from the way most of our ancestors related to them when they lived in small tribal or village cultures (a way of life that accounts for 90 percent of the time that human beings have been alive on Earth). The most striking difference is that we no longer see air, fire, water, stone, wood, and light as conscious, living beings vitally woven into the web of our lives. For many of us the elemental forms, shapes, and substances that make up the natural world are not manifestations of spirit. They are simply the environmental background.

In contrast to ancient legends about sleeping giants and dormant spirits waiting to be awakened from their slumber in the rocks and trees, it is we who are the slumbering giants. We wait to be called from sleep so that we can live our days fully awake and aware of both higher and deeper levels of reality. We hope for an expansion of consciousness that reveals the spirits in the rocks and trees that are far from dormant and still vitally spinning the wheels of life and playing the creative roles that have been theirs since the ancient times, before human beings emerged on the face of the Earth. Once awakened to the inner life of nature, we will live consciously and intelligently with the elemental beings as our ancestors did while performing simple daily tasks. Building fires, fetching water, chopping wood, preparing meals, and cleaning the hearth (or the modern equivalents of these tasks) will once again become sacred activities because we will recognize the spirits that participate with us in performing them.

DISCOVERING THE MIDDLE-WORLD JOURNEY

The middle-world journey into nonordinary realities can help us rekindle this intimate relationship with the spirits of nature. Just as the nonordinary realms found beneath the earth and above the sky open up alternate realities for the shaman, so too does the nonordinary realm of spirit overlaying the ordinary world in which we live our conscious lives. This is the "middle world" in the shaman's cosmos, and it too can be visited in shamanic states of consciousness.

Here are directions for a middle-world journey, based on those given in Chapter Three for lower- and upper-world journeys.

1. Lie on the floor; cover your eyes with a bandanna.

2. Repeat the intention or purpose of your journey to yourself three times.

3. Drummer begins to drum.

4. See yourself lying on the floor; call your power animal to join you; and tell it the purpose/destination of the journey.

5. See yourself and your power animal leaving the room through a window, a door, or (because you are traveling in spirit) a wall or roof.

6. When you reach the destination, fulfill the intention of the journey.

7. When the purpose for the journey is over or when the drumbeat calls you back, ask your power animal to escort you back to the place where you are lying.

8. Say goodbye to your power animal, and let your consciousness return to the room.

The method that power animals use for "escorting" a journeyer through a middle-world journey varies from power animal to power animal. Here are three of the most common ways.

- A power animal can help you fly or can carry you on its back as it flies into the sky and in the general direction of your destination. You rise too high, however, to see any of the actual landscape that you cross; but as you descend, you find yourself in the place you asked to go.

- A power animal can fly or carry you rapidly over the actual landscape between the place where your body lies and your destination, and you see it as you pass.

- A power animal can "whisk" you off in some fashion through a misty or foggy region and bring you out at the requested spot.

The important thing to remember is that when you arrive, you are arriving in the spiritual dimension of that place, not the actual physical locale. It may look somewhat different, as in a dream. The people and events that you see occurring there might not be occurring in ordinary reality at that moment, but what you see is a spiritual correspondence that carries the information or experience that you are seeking by going there. What this means is that you are not having a classic out-of-the-body experience, in which your soul or spirit leaves your body, traverses some distance, and sees the actual events that are taking place at that moment. It is possible that you *could* see what is actually going on in ordinary reality, but more than likely you will see some spiritual or metaphorical representation of it.

For example, I once did a journey to learn about my father's health. I journeyed to where he lives several states away and saw him energetically mowing the grass. I assumed he was feeling well. Later I called and asked how he was, and he confirmed that he was feeling fine. However, when I asked what he was doing at the time of the journey, he told me he was taking a nap. In other words, I hadn't seen what he was actually doing in ordinary reality. The spirits showed me a scene in the middle world that accurately gave me the information I wanted, but not what was actually going on. Had I seen my father taking a nap in the middle of the day, I might have assumed incorrectly that he was not feeling well.

The shamanic journey is not a classic out-of-the-body experience as we popularly define it: the soul leaving the body to wander temporarily through the ordinary realities of the world. The shamanic journey is still a journey in nonordinary reality, even though the middle-world journey is to a place that actually exists in ordinary reality. When we interact with people we see on a middle-world journey, we are dealing likewise with a spiritual reflection or some spiritual aspect of those people. When we check with those people later, they may have no conscious knowledge of our presence during the journey.

REASONS FOR DOING MIDDLE-WORLD JOURNEYS

The middle-world journey allows us to visit places and times that are important to us. We can go back in time and space to visit and relive the spiritual essence of events that took place long ago. As a spiritual practice, the middle-world journey can bring back memories of events that were important in our earlier spiritual development or allow us to make pilgrimages to sacred places for inspiration and renewal. A Catholic friend who had been a nun twenty years ago was suffering from a period of disillusionment with her current spiritual practices. She journeyed back to the convent she had been in and asked to see it as it was while she was living there. She roamed the halls, visited the chapel, said a prayer she used to love, talked to the other nuns whose spirits still imprinted the place, relived some important moments, and recaptured the religious fervor of her youth. Later she drew upon the experiences of this journey to energize her current spiritual life.

We can also use the middle-world journey to experience nature in its spirit forms and explore the natural areas where we live, to heighten our sense of the vital essences that flow through them. We can look at the Earth with our spirit eyes and see the energies that vibrate from it. We can listen with spirit ears to the songs that emanate from the forms and shapes that we ordinarily do not perceive as having voices. We can hear the music of the terrestrial spheres in which we live.

When we journey shamanically into a place that exists in ordinary reality we experience it on a more rarefied level: colors appear that we have no names for; the shapes of solid things become fluid and shift into other life forms; the spirit entities that dwell in the "hollowness" of physical reality appear and communicate with us. We see the blood and bones of the landscape over which we fly, through which we prowl, in which we swim. We exert our own spirit bodies, exercising our life's vital essence in a heightened atmosphere imbued with cosmic energy. In these ways we discover that the soils, waters, and winds of the biosphere, and all the life forms they support, are one ecological whole.

Here are some suggestions for typical middle-world journeys that let you experience distinct aspects of nature from a spiritual perspective.

- Journey just to bask in the sunlight in your backyard or the city park while in nonordinary reality.

- Do the same for moonlight on a lake.

- Journey into the wind and ride its trails of song.

- Gather with moisture in a cloud and fall as spring rain upon the earth.

- Journey to explore the various spirits that dwell in a nearby lake or pond.

- Journey to a tree, stream, or boulder, and sit before it, asking its spirit to come forth in some shape or form to meet you. Ask it to speak. Honor it, introduce yourself, ask it how you might be of service to it or to the environmental region where it lives.

- Journey to see, hear, or experience the "cosmic web" of energy that connects all the life forms and objects in a particular area, such as a valley, a city park, a hilltop.

These journeys can increase our capacity for the love of life that should characterize shamanic practice and deepen our faith in the sacredness of creation. Harvard zoologist and author E. O. Wilson calls this "biophilia" and exhorts us to adopt it as the much-needed stance required to face the overwhelming ecological crises that threaten life itself. What is "love of life"? Quite simply it is the awe, appreciation, respect, and admiration we have for all forms of life, whether animal, vegetable, or mineral. Wilson says, "To explore and affiliate with life is a deep and complicated process in mental development. Our existence depends on this propensity, our spirit is woven from it, hope rises on its currents." [1] Joyous middle-world journeys let us explore and affiliate with nature and its many communities of life. We return filled with the awe and appreciation of life that will keep our spirits hopeful and strengthen our commitment to the animistic values that shamanism imparts.

PLACES BETWIXT AND BETWEEN

An old folk saying found in many cultures is that magic occurs "betwixt and between" and under conditions that are "neither this, nor that." What is meant by "magic" is transformation, change, an alteration in the predictable flow of life accompanied by an alteration in the flow of our own consciousness. With the proper method and intention, we can send our altered consciousness or spirit to places betwixt and between the elements, places where the elemental spirits are engaged with each other, working their own magic, weaving their own spells. We can alter our consciousness so that it mingles with the consciousness of the elements, leaps the gulf between species, and bridges the space that separates us as physical beings.

Spiritual leaders among the Lakota Sioux have given us ways to think about this. In the words of Lame Deer, we "hop back and forth across the boundary line of the mind." [2] As Black Elk put it, we see "the spirit shapes of things." [3] Boundary lines and shapes, whether of the mind or of physical objects, alert us that we are operating on the "edge of things." We are in places where things begin and end, where objects touch each other, where auras blend, where energy is transferred. We are in the world of "betwixt and between," in realms that are "neither this, nor that."

The idea that a place or condition "betwixt and between" is magical has given rise to many interesting and popular clichés about magic and mystery. Like clichés in general, they contain kernels of truth. For example, the stroke of midnight is in neither the old day nor the new. Midnight, the "witching hour," is betwixt and between the days, a time of magic, mystery, and power. Even more compelling is the stroke of midnight on New Year's Eve—a moment in neither the old year nor the new—a time for wishes and resolutions to influence our fortune in the coming year.

Dawn and dusk are periods between day and night. They appear unannounced. By the time we notice that it is dawn, it has already been dawn for some time. The same is true for dusk. They seem to come from nowhere and at no measurable point in time. Twilight is a mysterious light, as the English word itself connotes—derived from "twin light"—a light that has a dual quality of both solar and lunar brightness, a mirror-like, magical light that partakes of both day and night. Twilight is also a time of magic. The air feels different, the "blue hour" arrives, and we enter the eerie time of not-day, not-night that will soon fade imperceptibly into night.

The Feast of November Eve, or Halloween, is traditionally a night that stands outside of time. As Samhain, the old Celtic new year, November Eve is in neither the old nor new year, and it is a night when the veil between the worlds of humans and spirits is lifted so that spirits can wander into our world and we into theirs. Even as a modern secular holiday, people continue to acknowledge Halloween as a time when we can walk "between the worlds" by dressing up in masks and costumes to hide our identities and allow ourselves to enter other worlds of consciousness and behavior far different from our own. We can join the world of the dead and the nether regions as skeletons, ghosts, goblins, faeries, gods and goddesses, witches and wizards, angels or devils. Cross-dressing as one's opposite gender or wearing animal skins and heads are ways to participate in the insubstantiality of this magical night, when shapeshifting is a common occurrence and things are not what they seem.

The magical quality of moonlight comes from the moon's betwixt-and-between status as a source of light. Although it generates no light of its own, the moon is nevertheless the night's major source of natural light, a borrowed light far removed from the sun in color and intensity. Moonlight is neither bright nor dark, and even though it allows us to see, it casts an obscure pallor on objects, making them easy to mistake for something other than what they are.

Traditionally the full moon is a powerful time for working magic, casting spells, and raising energy, but its fullness and power last only a moment. Although it appears round and full to the human eye for three successive nights, it begins to wane the moment it reaches fullness. For this reason, many workers of magic time their spells and rituals carefully to coincide with the exact minute the moon is full.

In the old Celtic calendar the night of the druid moon holds great power for ritual and ceremony. This moon occurs on the sixth night after the new moon appears in the western sky at sunset. It is the last night that the left edge of the moon will show a slight curve, the last night before the moon is half full. The druid moon marks the night between the two fortnights that make up the month: the darker fortnight when the moon is less than half full and when the three moonless nights occur, and the brighter fortnight when the moon is always more than half full and when the full moon itself occurs.

Fog, smoke, mist, and cloud have become dramatic clichés for magic and mystery because they are inherently shapeless and shifting in form and substance, and each is an ethereal composite of more than one element: air, water, heat, particle, and the light that passes through them. They are elusive wanderers and seem to belong to a world of their own, merely passing through ours. They are always verging on their own extinction, hanging onto a momentary existence in our visible world by the frailest of means. They disappear and leave no trace. Fog, smoke, mist, and cloud have become standard emblems of magic and the supernatural.

Irish poets believe that the edge of water—a shoreline, riverbank, or lakeside—is a place of otherworldly inspiration and visionary experiences. Here three worlds come together: air, water, and earth. The exact conjunction where one realm ends and another begins is not clearly discernible, for the line between them is continually changing with the ebb and flow of tides, the lapping of waves, the shifting of currents.

JOURNEYING BETWIXT AND BETWEEN

When we intentionally place our consciousness betwixt and between the elements, we are able to experience something of their magical or spiritual nature, their ability to reach out to each other, to change and be changed, to transform and be transformed. When we go between the wave and the beach, the fire and the log, the root and the soil, the bud and the stem, the drop of rain and the leaf, the blanket of new snow and the crust of old snow, we experience not only the transformations occurring between these elements, but the transformations that occur *intentionally and purposefully* between the elements and ourselves.

By being in spirit at these conjunctions of spirit and participating in the leap of energy, the dance of consciousness, we come to know the spirits of these elements in ways they know themselves. We begin to think like a river, see like a mountain, feel like a tree. We understand the intelligent nature of nonhuman beings in ways that we cannot fathom from the perspective of ordinary awareness. We then realize our kinship with the natural elements and discover that there is no separation between us and them on the spiritual level.

The Chewong people in Malaysia believe that every species has its own *med mesign*, or set of eyes, allowing each to see in a different way. They believe that the perceptions of all animals and species are true, the human perception being just one among many. In fact, the Chewong do not have a term that means the "nonhuman" world. Humans and nonhumans are part of a whole.[4] We should adapt this view to our shamanic practice, and then journey, as Chewong shamans do, between the worlds of reality where other species and elements dwell to see the world with their eyes and experience life as they do.

Here is a middle-world journey technique to become aware of the deeper levels of activity going on among the natural elements. There are two parts to this process. The first is a preparatory stage to allow our awareness to experience the betwixt-and-between state within ourselves, a kind of "revving up" of consciousness, so to speak. In the second stage we send our consciousness out from our own energy fields to the combined fields of energy between two or more elements, where we experience the transformation that is taking place between those elements. In shamanic terms, we are sending our spirits out to participate and communicate with the spirits in nature.

Before you begin, light a candle. Then place a rock about the size of your fist in a small bowl and fill the bowl with water. Place the bowl and candle on the floor and sit about eight to ten feet away from them.

Keep your eyes closed during both stages: during stage one while you are focusing on your breathing and during stage two when you journey out to the place between the elements. Even though the elements are in front of you, you are working in an altered state of consciousness and it helps to close your eyes and block out distractions from ordinary reality.

STAGE ONE: THE PLACES BETWEEN OUR BREATHS

In stage one you will become aware of the "betwixt and between" places in your breathing. Here is how to do it.

1. Slow your breathing down, take deeper, more complete breaths, and notice the points at the top and bottom of each breath. These are the points where the inhale turns into an exhale and where the exhale becomes the next inhale. Both are places of transformation.

2. As you breathe, do not hold your breath or pause at these points, or you will turn them into fixed places and they will lose their insubstantial quality of being "neither this, nor that." To pause would be like stopping the clock at the stroke of midnight in an attempt to make midnight last. So allow each inhale to flow naturally into the exhale, and vice versa.

3. Without pausing, notice what it feels like when you become conscious of these spots, even as you move gently through and beyond them. Try to experience them as places outside of time and space, as conditions that are composed of *neither* the act of inhaling *nor* the act of exhaling (nor, obviously, the act of pausing).

4. Take at least ten breaths to experience repeatedly the elusive quality of being betwixt and between.

5. After approximately ten breaths, try to find words to describe the experience. You may find this difficult to do because you are trying to describe something that is indescribable, perhaps ineffable, a quasi-mystical experience that defies definition or words. But try.

In teaching this technique I enjoy noticing the kinds of imagery that people use to describe this experience, especially images that indicate the encounter with opposites. One woman said, "I felt the place between inhaling and exhaling was a place of tremendous emptiness." Another person said it was like "a cosmic void." On the other hand, some people discover a fullness there. "It's like the fullness, the totality." A young man thought it was "dark there between breaths," while his girlfriend got a flash of "yellow light" each time she passed through the spot. Some feel the place between breaths is immense; others find it very narrow, even claustrophobic. Some people experience total freedom as they pass through it; others feel trapped. "Each time I get there, I'm glad to get into the next half of my breath," said one person.

People who do not experience one half of a duality often have an experience that transcends duality. Their descriptions suggest the place between breaths is crowded with possibilities, a yin-yang field of infinite choices, a no-place hanging on the edge of becoming a real place, the "start of something big."

What does this suggest besides the fact that people will experience the same thing in different ways? I think that each person is trying to express the mystical sensations that occur when we place our conscious awareness in a place of transformation, where one thing is turning into another—and in the case of breathing, literally each half of the breath is turning into its polar or opposite half. When consciousness moves outside of space and time (as we usually experience space and time), we are between the worlds of being and nonbeing where shapeshifting occurs, where things experience and realize their opposites, where there is no duality. But as we try to bring that experience back into the world of duality and describe it, we inevitably choose words that indicate our encounter with duality, even though those words may describe only half the polarity. So we say the place betwixt and between is dark or light, empty or full, immense or narrow. In reality, it is no-place, where the human mind can meet anything, or its opposite, and transcend one or the other, or both.

After you have practiced this stage one several times and tried to refine your descriptions of what it feels like betwixt and between your breaths, you are ready to use stage one as a launching process for stage two.

STAGE TWO: THE PLACES BETWEEN THE ELEMENTS

The second stage of this practice is to send your consciousness away from your own field of energy to mingle with the consciousness of two of the elements in front of you, where they are actively engaged with each other: either between the water and the rock or between the flame and the wick. Here is the method for doing this.

1. Before you begin observing your breaths, decide whether you wish to send your spirit to the place between the rock and the water or the flame and the wick. In this way you will not have to interrupt your practice by making a decision. Let's say you have chosen the place between the rock and the water.

2. After you have observed about ten breaths as described above, send your attention, consciousness, or spirit (however you wish to think of it) out to the place betwixt and between the rock and the

water, those spaces between the atoms, where their energy blends, where their auras meet, where their spirits are engaged in the dance of life.

3. Hold your consciousness out there between the rock and the water for as long as you can.

4. Then withdraw it into yourself again.

5. Focus on your breathing again, observe one or two complete breaths, and then open your eyes.

It is important to consciously send your spirit *out from you* to the place between the rock and water, rather than just *think about* the space between the rock and water. These are really two different kinds of awareness, and with practice you will understand the difference quite clearly. If you merely *think about* the place betwixt and between, you will not experience its transformational quality. The magical or mystical impact of the experience will elude you.

You may discover that you can't stay out there for more than a few seconds at first. With practice you will be able to stay there for longer periods of time. Practice both sets of elements: water and rock, fire and wick. Experience how each is different.

On your first forays outward to the elements, your experience might be best classified as simply a "mood" or an atmosphere that feels different because you have moved into an energy field created and shared by nonhuman elements. You bring with you your own energy and mood (a combination of thoughts and feelings), but when your energy mingles with the energies of rock and water, the experience is noticeably alien to what you are accustomed.

Repeat this practice with the rock and water and flame and wick over a period of a few days, and try to describe your sensations *between* and *with* the elements more accurately each time.

DRUMMING YOUR WAY BETWEEN THE ELEMENTS

You don't need to use the drum to send your spirit between the elements, but light drumming can help, particularly when you want to extend your stay out there. As with the shamanic journey, monotonous drumming or what is called "sonic driving" alters consciousness, focuses the attention, and creates a sense of excitement and urgency. As shamans put it, they "ride" their drums. You can do this drumming for yourself. You can also use a rattle.

The pattern for drumming or rattling is as follows:

1. For the first stage, drum gently and softly in a heartbeat pattern. The heartbeat and breathing rhythms complement each other nicely.

2. When you send your consciousness out to the elements, change to the faster journey beat with a slight increase in volume. The drumming does not have to be very loud because this kind of middle-world journey is not as far or deep as a journey into the lower or upper worlds, and your spirit does not travel very far from that part of you that remains conscious of ordinary reality. A light, gentle beat is sufficient.

3. When you are ready to return, resume the heartbeat pattern again and pull your spirit back into your body.

4. Observe your breathing for two or three breaths before opening your eyes.

PRACTICING OUTDOORS

Once you have acquired some facility moving into the space between the water and rock and the flame and wick, try sending your consciousness to elements outside your home. You can do this in two ways, either by sending your spirit out while you stay seated indoors or by actually going outside and sitting near the elements you plan to merge with. Urban practitioners can journey while indoors to places they have visited in the country or that they know from former outings into natural settings.

There are two approaches for sending your spirit to a place outdoors while you remain physically indoors. You can send your spirit to a specific place you already know, such as a particular rock along a river bank or the root of a specific oak tree up the hill. Or you can decide on the kind of elements you want to journey to, such as water and rock, but leave your specific destination open-ended. In other words, send your spirit to the river and allow it to find a rock, or send your spirit up the hill and allow it to zero in on a tree.

Whether you stay indoors or go out, keep your eyes closed to block out distractions just as you did when you practiced before the candle and bowl of water. In time you may discover that under certain conditions you can keep your eyes open without being distracted. Situations that are mesmerizing in themselves, such as logs burning in the fireplace, sunlight reflecting on water, or waves crashing on a beach, have a way of blocking out other sights and sounds. In these situations you may be able to keep your eyes open or half open. You might try beginning with them open, closing them later, and reopening them again when it feels right.

LOCAL SPIRITS AND COSMIC SPIRITS

As you practice journeying betwixt and between in various outdoor settings, you begin to discern several things. First, the spirit of one element—say, water—has a kind of Oversoul or generic spiritual quality that you will discover whenever and wherever you merge with it. It is something like a prototype of that element, a natural essence. But you will also meet very specific and unique local water spirits—in ponds, rivers, streams, waterfalls, rain puddles—which have their own characteristics and personalities.

Our ancestors were keenly aware of this, judging from their knowledge of various local deities that ruled specific wells, springs, and rivers, each with its own name, personality, and rites. These local deities were different from each other yet related, just as they were distinguishable from yet related to the higher water deities, such as a God of the Storm or the Goddess of the Sea. In spite of the differences, local water spirits and major water deities share some common essence and existence with the Oversoul of Water. You will find the same is true of other elements: fire, wind, soil, rock, plants, trees.

One morning while camping in Pennsylvania, I woke early to see a magnificent purple mist rising from the lake near my campsite. It was achingly beautiful, and I found myself not able to resist watching it. Some voice seemed to call me from within it, so I closed my eyes, took several slow, deep breaths, and sent my spirit out to the place betwixt and between the lake's surface and the mist. I found myself in the region where infinitesimally small particles of moisture were lifting themselves off the water and ascending into the morning air. I rose with them and then descended, and played in the air and water. To this day I can remember that mist. It was unlike any other mist I have ever known anywhere else. It had a uniqueness, individuality, soul.

As you travel, you will meet river spirits, rock spirits, tree spirits, and hill spirits in various places, and you will sense something familiar about each one because you have encountered a kindred spirit elsewhere. Having once met the local spirits of a place, you can journey back to them again or call them to join you wherever you are, even in the city. For years I have had a personal relationship with the spirits of certain springs and mountains in the Missouri Ozarks where I have gone for vision quests and days of prayer and reflection (not to mention canoeing and camping trips with friends). I still journey in spirit to them regularly, even though I live more than a thousand miles away.

INVITATIONS AND REFUSALS

There are times you may feel that your spirit cannot join the elements. You try to journey outward to the places betwixt and between, but you cannot get there. You feel blocked or repelled, or you can't find the "place" between the elements at all. You can interpret this in several ways. Quite simply, you may not be up for it because you are tired or too distracted by other thoughts. The time or setting is not right.

It's also possible the elements themselves may not want you to join them at that moment for whatever reasons that are unique to them and which you may never know. We should accept and respect such moments. This doesn't mean you cannot join them later, maybe as soon as a few minutes later. But we should accept the notion that spirits have activities, times, circumstances, and "schedules" that do not include us. We should not intrude. We must always do this exercise with the utmost respect.

Sending our spirits into the places between the elements, rather than directly into the elements themselves, is respectful and non-intrusive, allowing the spirits to turn us away as we approach if the time is not appropriate for this kind of merging. It is like stepping out onto the dance floor where the spirits are dancing, and waiting to see if they will invite you to join them. Sometimes they will; other times they may not. So wait it out.

You may also discover that although you send your spirit into a place between two elements, one element seems to draw you into it more than the other, as the mist in Pennsylvania pulled me into it rather than the lake. I always take this as a sign that one element wants to share its experience with me for some reason, and I enter more deeply into communion with that element, merge with it, allow my consciousness to shapeshift into it. The other element may make the overtures next time.

Arriving at a place betwixt and between is not always the final destination. You may find there a portal or entryway into interior worlds within the elements. We may discover that they are opening "the world within themselves" to our fuller understanding. In the "Mountains and Waters Sutra," a Buddhist text, we read,

It is not only that there is water in the world, but there is a world in water. It is not just in water. There is a world of sentient beings in clouds. There is a world of sentient beings in the air. There is a world of sentient beings in fire...There is a world of sentient beings in a blade of grass." [5]

This is similar to what the Celts mean by the "Hollow Hills." There are palaces of light, glorious landscapes, otherworldly colors and fragrances, and radiant beings within the hills. And not just the hills. Everything—water, air, clouds, fire, a blade of grass—has an interior nature, a hidden realm, into which we, as shamanic practitioners, can find the entrance. Journeying beyond the limitations of ego and ordinary consciousness by going betwixt and between the elements is one of those methods for discovering the invisible entries into the Otherworld.

INNOVATIONS, APPLICATIONS, AND THE ETHICS OF IT ALL

A few winters ago a friend lost twenty trees on her property when devastating storms swept the area. As a shamanic practitioner she was quite upset the next day to walk the land and see so many trees that were like old friends to her lying uprooted, twisted, dead. She felt as if they had been slaughtered. It was important to her to know what they felt and where their spirits were. She journeyed into places around them, where soil still clung to roots, where leaves hung half torn and crumbled, where one trunk lay across another. She located places betwixt and between, sent her spirit there, and spent time with the spirits of many of those trees as root, bark, limb, trunk. She discovered some interesting things.

"Some of the trees did not mind being uprooted," she told me. They explained to her that their life force would continue in different forms, that the soil where they had stood and lived would still contain some of their energy; even their physical remains would provide sources of life for other creatures. One tree told her, "Dying is changing form, moving on, doing other things." Another said, "It's part of God's plan." Other trees, however, expressed a kind of regret for having their lives cut short.

Like a young person facing death, they wanted more time. For them the storm disrupted some kind of contentment or happiness. But they too said that life did not end with the storm. In some form or other, their physical bodies would be recycled back into nature.

I know an artist who sends her consciousness betwixt and between the light and her subject—say an apple—and picks up the mood or feel of being there, absorbing the color, texture, and form. Then she places her consciousness at the tip of her brush, between the paint on the canvas and the paint on the brush. As she does so, she recreates the experience of being with the apple by bringing the mood and feel of that experience into her attention as she paints. In this way she transfers her spiritual knowledge of her subject to the paint and ultimately to the canvas. She explained to me, "I instruct my brush, the paint, the canvas to recreate the apple. If they ask how, I tell them my spirit will guide them."

Health-care providers can use this form of journeying to encourage healing. A chiropractor, for example, routinely sends his consciousness to the place in the vertebrae where he plans to make an adjustment. He uses one or two breaths to prepare his consciousness, watching the places between inhaling and exhaling, and then with the next exhale, he moves his spirit into the patient's back. "I put my attention and intention between the parts of the spine that are out of line, and my spirit says to them, 'Okay, guys, it's time to get back in place.'" Then he administers the adjustment.

The principle involved in journeying betwixt and between for healing purposes has implications in other areas as well. In fact, the traditional notion of magic spells—causing something to happen in nature by transforming consciousness or using unseen powers—should make us pause and ask, "When is it ethical to use magical or spiritual power to cause change for your own purposes?"

Let's use the classic example of weather magic: a spell either to bring or ward off rain.

We can journey betwixt and between the clouds, and sometimes influence them into bringing rain if we need it or passing us by without raining. This is not the same thing as controlling the weather, although the popular perception is that that is what happens (when it works). As shamanic practitioners we do not control the spirits, but if we routinely journey to them and spend time with them, we build up relationships with them. We become friends or allies. We have influence. When the cause is right and our intention is for the good of all concerned, and we treat the spirits of nature with respect, we can often persuade them to grant our requests, whether it be for a sunny day or for a realignment of pinched vertebrae.

It is vitally important to keep our intentions pure. Shamanic techniques are just tools that can be used for good or harm. In most cultures there is a belief that someone who becomes corrupted by psychic or spiritual power and misuses it to do harm will suffer the same harm, sometimes threefold. It is also widely held that a person who misuses spiritual power will soon lose that power. Spirit allies will no longer cooperate. Power animals will leave. So we should take utmost care not to try to influence the spirits for purely selfish or vengeful reasons. If we cannot honestly state at the beginning of any magical work, "I ask that this be done for the greatest good of the greatest number of people most directly involved, and that it harm none," then we should not work the magic. Or, we should ask that the magic not work!

It would be good for us to follow the practice of many tribal shamans who routinely ask the spirits to take pity on them and grant their request. An attitude of humility can remind us that it is not we who have power, but the spirits. We are only partners, dependent on their cooperation and good graces for our success. We do not control the spirits, we merely participate with them.

TAKING INSTRUCTION FROM THE SPIRITS OF NATURE

Our ability to communicate with the spirits of nature is not solely for our own benefit. The spirit world needs us as much as we need it. Religious literature from around the world is filled with episodes of angels and other spirits instructing humans to undertake important tasks and go on dangerous missions for some higher goal. The lesser spirits—the elementals and nature devas—may also have requests, although most likely not as dramatic. Nevertheless, reciprocity is a key theme in the encounters between spirits and mortals in almost all cultures. Communication between the worlds is a true two-way dialogue.

A practical application, for example, is gardening. Before you plant a garden, journey to various areas to find the spots most conducive for specific flowers or vegetables. Go between rock and soil in one corner of the garden with the intention of learning what kind of plant would thrive best there, or what type would not do well. Before you put the plants in the ground, journey to them in their pots or go between the seeds, and ask what section of the garden would be most suitable for them. Take their suggestions, and plant accordingly.

Once the garden is planted, you can communicate with the garden devas periodically by sending your spirit to the place between the soil and root or sunlight and leaf to ask what the plants and soil need. They may need fertilizer, more water, less water, looser soil, special ingredients. Gardening this way is an excellent practice for creating a partnership with nature right in your backyard. And it works. Results show that treating plants as conscious, intelligent beings invariably produces better, healthier crops. Plants tend to grow better or faster when humans acknowledge them, speak to them, sing for them.

As mentioned above, when you feel a particular element drawing you to it more than the other, respond accordingly and find out what it wants. It may want to teach you something. A Siberian shaman named Sereptie tells of his spirit teacher continually giving him the same advice whenever he asked to know something: "Find it out! Find it out!"[6] The exhortation was for Sereptie to journey directly to the spirits of nature and the elements and ask them. It's as simple as that: ask them.

From a shamanic point of view we can acquire information, advice, or instructions from anything in nature, because everything is alive and wants to communicate. George Russell, an Irish poet and mystic known by the pen name A. E., who lived at the turn of the last century, described a revelation he had one day lying on a hillside and realizing the intelligence and consciousness within nature: "Every flower was a word, a thought. The grass was speech; the trees were speech; the waters were speech; the winds were speech." [7] The well-being of the planet—flowers, grass, trees, wind, water, and us—depends on our being able to hear that speech, and to respond.

WORD IS OUT

Over time, word will go out among the spirits in your environment that you are someone who reaches out to the spirit world, and you will get a reputation of being friendly, cooperative, worth knowing. There are countless stories in tribal cultures as well as among European peasant communities about how the faery folk and local land spirits routinely appear to help, advise, protect, and socialize with certain individuals. In the British Isles, for example, there are many accounts of people being helped by faeries and spirits. In some places, spirits called "brownies" will help with household chores. Some spirits leave gold coins for their friends. Other spirits help herd cows and protect private homes by scaring away intruders.

And who are these individuals who are blessed with such friends? Usually people who take the spirit folk seriously, who have the "faery faith," who leave gifts for the "good people." They are men and women who honor the wishes and needs of the nonhuman world. If the spirits interacted with humans more frequently in years gone by, it was because there were more people who believed in them, respected them, and paid homage to them. These people were our own ancestors who survived for millennia with, and because of, a profound respect for the nonhuman forces of nature.

Our shamanic practice should include prayers to the spirits of the elements, similar to those said by our ancestors. As models we can use the prayers, chants, and invocations collected in nineteenth-century Scotland and Ireland. These prayers covered daily activities such as milking cows, building fires in the morning and banking them at night, weaving cloth, setting tables, caring for the sick. Virtually every chore of the day was perceived as an occasion for calling upon God, the saints or angels, ancient gods and goddesses, or the spirits of nature themselves. These prayers and invocations have familiar echoes in the prayers and chants still used by indigenous people to accompany their daily work.

For example, a Scottish prayer to cure a chest pain begins:

Power of moon have I over you,
Power of sun have I over you,
Power of rain have I over you,
Power of dew have I over you....[8]

It continues mentioning power from sea, land, stars, planets, universe, skies, saints, and heaven. The supplicant calls on the powers present in nature and clearly expects them to hear and respond to the request to pull the chest pain out of the ailing person.

The Irish still say this morning prayer composed by Saint Patrick:

I arise today
Through the strength of heaven—
Light of sun,
Radiance of moon,
Splendour of fire,
Speed of lightning,
Swiftness of wind,
Depth of sea,
Stability of earth,
Firmness of rock.[9]

The sentiments expressed in this prayer undoubtedly go back well into pre-Christian times, for Patrick is saying that the "strength of heaven" is to be found in sun, moon, fire, lightning, wind, sea, earth, and rock. At the heart of this prayer is an animistic, druidic view of Creation: that the Creator's power is immanent and accessible to us.

Last, a simple wish for someone reads as follows:

Power of raven be yours,
Power of eagle be yours,
Power of the Fiann [a band of Irish heroes].

Power of storm be yours,
Power of moon be yours,
Power of sun.

Goodness of sea be yours,
Goodness of earth be yours,
Goodness of heaven.[10]

These prayers and charms should have a familiar ring to us because on some deeper level of consciousness we intuitively respond to the numinous presence and power of nature. It's almost impossible to recite these simple statements of faith without awakening some half-slumbering memory that the conscious life stream flowing through the elements can be summoned by the mere act of calling on the spirits of those elements. We can call them by name—sun, moon, rain, dew, wind, storm—or simply call on the "God of the Elements" as the Irish and Scots do. The Spirit or spirits within the elements become our helping spirits, bestowing protection, power, peace, or healing. When we consciously acknowledge their role in our lives, our tasks become imbued with the power and presence of sacred beings. It is not we alone who build a fire: we, the fuel, and *Fire* build a fire.

We must rekindle this kind of faith today by laying aside our skepticism and by weaving into our lives ways to interact with nature so that we become aware of how densely populated it is with the "invisible folk" who reside in the fields, streams, and wooded areas of the natural world.

Middle-world journeys, conscious merging with the elements of nature, and prayers like these can put us on this path. The spirits will begin to take the initiative and appear and communicate with us of their own accord. In time, we become so aware of them that it is truly second nature for us to know what they are up to.

FINDING OUR TRUE NATURE

Spending conscious time with the spirits of the elements is a revitalizing spiritual experience because the elements always know what they are created to do and they do it. They have no doubts, worries, suspicions, uncertainty, or reluctance. How unlike us! Much of our day, if not most, is spent fretting over what we should do. We flit back and forth between "shoulds" and "shouldn'ts," trying to make up our minds. A genuine spiritual experience frees us from uncertainty because it shows us our true nature, our real self, by giving us glimpses of how our real self can operate when we step outside our petty ego concerns and enter the secret life of wind, fire, water, stone, wood, plants, and sunlight. As we become aware of who and what they are, and are meant to be, we feel exhilarated and confident that we too were created to share in this same state of being. Like the elements, we were created for a purpose. Things make sense.

We all long for this kind of numinous experience. It is the jewel of great worth that the mystic possesses in moments of unity with divine power. On a lesser scale, merging with the elements of nature places us in reach of that same confident knowing: We realize who we are, why we are here, what we are meant to do—by participating with fellow creatures who exhibit this same genuineness and certitude.

At such moments, we also feel at home in nature, as we are meant to feel, as our shamanic ancestors once felt. Even when we send our spirits into a forest fire, thundering storm clouds, or the fiercely swirling rapids of a flooded river, we experience a peace and tranquillity that comes from being true to nature, of being with the spirit in nature as it is true to itself. At the center of even the most violent natural phenomenon there is a sense of calm and composure, a peace that comes from acting in accordance with one's natural design. By being on intimate terms with the elements, we learn that we, like they, can be true to our nature. We can also learn how to be true to *their* nature and participate consciously with them in the beauty, harmony, and divine purpose of creation.

CHAPTER SIX

SPIRITS OF PLACE

Sometimes when walking through woods on a path or track I have never explored before, I will get the distinct feeling that I am being watched, as if I have stumbled into some private lair, a sanctuary protected by a guardian spirit who knows I have entered. I usually consider my options: turn around and run; keep walking but speed it up; sit down and surrender. Over the years I have used all three tactics.

Power spots, or sacred areas, or the thin places between the worlds—call them what you will—often unsettle us this way. In fact, in some native traditions this is the way you know you have found a power spot: the Power or the Presence that inhabits the area is too strong to ignore; you know you have stepped into a domain where the energy is powerful, where you may even feel threatened, where you might not belong—where you are being *watched.*

This is a more intense "watching" than what you might experience normally in nature. The Koyukon people in Alaska, for example, believe that the forest has eyes and routinely watches human activity. All things, in the Koyukon perspective, are endowed with human-like qualities and take an interest in the health and well-being of the region where they live. Shamanic practitioners often sense this watching and observing as they become more aware of spirit activity in nature. The feeling of being watched when you enter a sacred place is usually more intense and unsettling. You become aware of the Dwellers whose territory you have entered. You may even have a sense of danger.

The Dwellers whose spiritual presence protects the physical landscape mean us no harm, and following the example of our tribal ancestors, we do well to get to know them and ally ourselves with them, for we share environments. Some spirit Dwellers are literally our next-door neighbors, our landmates with whom our lives are intertwined as we work and play on the same soil. Others dwell in more distant areas we may only visit on occasion or stumble upon once in a lifetime. In this chapter we will look at ways to acknowledge and honor the spirits of place both at home and afar, create appropriate relationships with them, and discover how to root our shamanic practice in the ground and roots of ordinary reality.

Historically, tribal shamans lived most of their lives within a limited circumference extending only a few miles from the village. Even the more nomadic tribes that moved back and forth between summer and winter quarters still spent most of their days within well-known landscapes and physical environments. For them, the spirits of nature were not generic nature spirits of oak, waterfall, ocean, or mountain, but the familiar and specific spirits of *this* oak, *this* waterfall, *this* ocean, and *this* mountain. These spirits had local, native names and were familiar to the people, especially to shamans who called upon these deities to help them in their spiritual and healing work.

As shamanic practitioners we need to strengthen our own activities with the power of specific Dwellers in the invisible realms around our places of home and work, and in the more distant sites we hold sacred for the spiritual energy they bestow upon us when we visit them.

GEOMANTIC JOURNEYS

At the heart of this practice of communing with spirits of place is the ancient science and art of geomancy. Literally the term means "to divine the Earth spirit." Here "divine" means to discover, locate, or perceive intuitively—all essential activities for shamanic practitioners. The goal is to create conscious relationships with land spirits in order to create conscious and intimate relationships with the environment itself. In any natural area there are various forms of life sharing the soil, air, water, and other resources. A simple book on ecology with good illustrations or photographs will show the myriad creatures, great and small, who live with—and off—each other in any bioregion. In every swath of landscape, therefore, we can expect to meet a host of spirits: animal, plant, and elemental.

In our own backyards and fields or deep in the woods and distant valleys, there is often a particular spirit who dominates the region. In some areas several spirits may cooperatively rule. Usually you can tell by just looking around: a particularly large tree or outcrop of rock, a predominant hilltop, a persistently babbling creek or waterfall—any of these might be a candidate for the primary guardian spirit of a particular place. But allow for the possibility that the main spirits, perhaps the oldest spirits, the elders of a given place, are not the most physically obvious. They might be smaller beings living within the root systems or in the pebbles of the creek bed, or they might be larger spirits who encompass the greater area—the spirit of the valley itself, the spirit of the entire mountain.

One way for you to meet the spirit of a particular place is to embark on a middle-world journey in which you ask your power animal to introduce you to that spirit. The spirit may appear to you in human or animal form, or possibly some other shape or quality. You can tell your power animal that you would like to meet the spirit in a certain form if you wish, or leave it up to the spirit to appear in the shape that is appropriate for you and it.

Approach the spirit with your request to get to know it, learn from it, and honor it in appropriate ways both in nonordinary and ordinary realities. You can ask very practical questions such as how to maintain certain land, what to plant in a garden, what kind of care particular trees might need, how to develop an area that you plan to restore or landscape. The human need for "landscape development" is not a sign of modern perverseness as some critics have claimed; all societies reshape the land to some extent, use it, and leave a mark of some kind. What's important is to do this work respectfully and with a sincere desire to enhance and honor the land, the other creatures who live on it, and all the spirits of the place.

Another method for meeting a spirit of a place is to use the betwixt-and-between method explained in the previous chapter. Here is a way of doing this to meet the spirit of a small self-contained place, such as a grove or creek bed.

1. Use a small drum or rattle, because these sounds are traditional ways to call spirits. They will also cover outdoor noises and help to keep your awareness focused.

2. While sitting at the spot, select a place betwixt and between that involves the land feature whose spirit you want to meet. For example, if the feature is an oak, focus on the place between the root and the soil; for a creek, select a place between a rock and the water.

3. Observe the betwixt places in your breathing for a few minutes to prepare.

4. When you feel ready, send your consciousness into the place in nature with the request that the element or feature that is the spirit of the place respond to you in some way that begins a dialogue or a merging so that you can learn from it.

5. When you have ended your engagement with the spirit, thank it, and withdraw back into yourself.

To encounter the spirit of a large area, such as the spirit of a valley, mountain, gorge, or bay, you can adapt the betwixt-and-between method as follows.

1. Become very aware of your presence in the area: where you are sitting, the view of the landscape in each direction, the location of trees, outcrops, boulders, hills, and so forth.

2. Choose two features between which you are sitting. Let's say they are the lake on your left and a mountain range to your right. Then close your eyes.

3. Watch the betwixt places in your breathing as you prepare.

4. When you feel ready to go betwixt and between the lake and the mountain range, instead of sending your consciousness or spirit outwards to a specific point in the usual way, allow your spirit (think of it as your aura) to expand until it is much larger than yourself, perhaps as large as a tree.

5. As you expand, call the spirits of the lake and mountain range to join you as you sit between them. You will feel one or both of them "close in" around you, "crowding" you a bit with their presence. You may even begin to sense that they are gigantic (as are you at the moment).

6. Continue to be there with them, just as you would hang out betwixt and between elements in a smaller space.

7. At some point when you feel comfortable with them, ask them to let you meet the spirit of the entire area of which they are a part. You might discover that the two feature-spirits fade out or shapeshift into one spirit who is the spirit of the place. Spend time with that spirit, getting to know it as you would on a standard journey.

8. When finished, thank the spirits, and withdraw your consciousness back into yourself.

TEACHERS OF THE NATURAL LIFE

In the ancient Greek world, tree and water spirits were called dryads and naiads, respectively. These were usually encountered as small spirits dwelling in groves of trees or in creeks, rivers, and springs. In western and northern Europe and in Ireland and the British Isles, the male and female spirits of the wild also played a major role in ancient spiritual life as the Green Man of the Forest and the Woman of the Sacred Waters. Green Men were often seen as wild creatures, covered with shaggy hair, horned or antlered, or sometimes having leaves, moss, grass, and vines instead of hair and beard. In the popular imagination they were frightening to behold and encounter.

In Arthurian lore, the Green Knight who can cut off his own head and put it back on is a variation of the Green Man, still exemplifying nature's ability to die each winter and return to life with the spring. In the Fenian legends of Ireland the Guragach, or woodland churl, is a type of wild, hairy Green Man who, like the Green Knight, challenges warriors to contests of beheading, knowing that he can pick up his severed head and place it back on his shoulders.

The Women of the Sacred Waters might be goddesses or spirits of rivers, springs, wells, or lakes. The ancient Europeans viewed the natural sources of water, places where water emerged from the earth, as entries into the Otherworld. The guardians of these portals tended to be female. People offered gifts to the Spirits of the Waters, sacrificing weapons, tools, money, and jewelry in exchange for healing or good fortune. The Lady of the Lake who gave Arthur the sword Excalibur is but one example of how these water goddesses bestowed power and assistance upon humans. The water from certain wells, springs, and sacred lakes, such as that at Lourdes in France, is still revered as having magical or healing properties. Such places are often still under the protection of a female spirit.

Whatever their appearance or demeanor, whether friendly or frightening, our ancestors knew the Green Men and the Women of the Waters as the spirits or deities of the wild vegetation typical of the forests and uncultivated fields and the water upon which that vegetation depended. The Desana people, who live along the tributaries of the Amazon in Colombia, have a similar perspective. They view the Earth as composed of land and water. The lush wild vegetation of their tropical homeland is considered to be male energy, while the slow rivers that meander through it are seen as female energy. As described by David Suzuki and Peter Knudtson, the two forces are "opposing but complementary." In the Desana world view "a forest, intrinsically masculine, is locked in a reciprocal embrace with the river, feminine in its flows, that courses through it…(spawning) countless shifting and subtle interactions, creations, and obligations within the natural world, of which humankind is an integral part." [1]

As you meet the spirit of a specific place, you might ask it to appear as a Green Man or a Woman of the Waters, allowing it to take the garb and guise that it chooses. In my own practice, I know a Green Man and a Woman of the Waters who are the spirits of a place in the Missouri Ozarks, but neither looks at all traditional: no vegetation in place of hair, no gossamer gown, just a man and a woman, the masculine and feminine energies causing life, growth, death, decay, and rebirth in the web of life holding together that region of the ancient Ozarks.

Asking the spirits to come to you in particular shapes and guises is always done with the intention to deal with them more comfortably so that you can speak to them, get to know them, and be able to call upon them for help and instruction. If you ask them to appear in "traditional or classical" forms and it is not appropriate for them to do so (or for you to see them that way), they will not. Ask your power animal about these matters, and express honestly why you feel the need to know certain spirits in certain ways. Then trust the spirits who are your helpers to do what is right for you at this stage in your spiritual development.

One of the reasons for having a Green Man or a Woman of the Waters as a spirit advisor is to learn how to live the natural life. The very phrase "natural life" may not ring many bells for some of us. What is a natural life today? Does it mean living closer to nature and animals? Does it mean going to bed with the sun? Does it mean no videos? Most of us live with technological conveniences that transform—or even eliminate—our encounters with the elements, seasons, weather patterns, animals, and so forth. Would the natural life require leaving the city and moving to the country? Or does it mean just getting out of urban environments once in a while to go for a hike in the woods or desert? For each of us, the answer may be slightly or decidedly different.

Journey to the Green Man and the Woman of the Waters to ask how you can lead a more natural life. In fact, it is good to do this journey in each season or several times a year whenever we feel that our style of living is becoming less "natural" and more dependent upon places and things that seem disconnected to the Earth's rhythms and patterns. While there may be nothing inherently incompatible between urbanized or technologized environments and shamanic practice, we still need to stay connected to the deeper energies and rhythms of the Earth that are embedded in our psyches and in our genetic inheritance from past generations. The lure into a totally un-nature-like lifestyle is hard to resist in a culture like ours that glamorizes the latest technology, fashions, and trends in modern living. As shamanic practitioners we need to keep our spiritual roots firmly planted and watered in the mysteries of the Earth. Green Man and Woman of the Sacred Waters can help.

One January as I was walking down a country road, Green Man suddenly overtook me and walked alongside. I asked him, "What are you doing?" He answered, "Being winter." Then he asked, "What are *you* doing?" I realized almost instantly that "Being winter" should be my answer also, but I wasn't "being winter" at all. I was daydreaming about how the apple orchards I was passing through would look in the spring blossom-time, not cluttered with the cut branches that were recently pruned and still lying in clumps between the rows. I have a tendency when winter seems like too much to bear to start fantasizing about spring. But Green Man was right as usual. I needed to "be winter," and so I journeyed to him over the next few weeks to get instructions on how to "winterize" my soul and live more contentedly within the seasonal mysteries of the moment. He taught me how to find value in boringly gray days, sub-zero temperatures, and cancellations due to blizzards. Unfortunately, he wasn't able to teach me how to kick up my heels and *enjoy* these things that are so valuable!

RECOGNIZING A POWER SPOT

We each have different abilities to detect Earth energies and respond to them, just as we each have different abilities to feel the energy in crystals and sacred stones. I'm not a person who can pick up a crystal and go into raptures over the energies coming from it, even though everyone else who handled it is swooning. In fact, I hate to admit it, but I usually don't feel anything too remarkable in stones, except the ones that have some personal significance for me. On the other hand, I can get high just from catching a glimpse of a creek or brook when I drive down a road. There's something about the sudden appearance of flowing water that makes my heart beat faster. And when I drive across a bridge over a river, I often swerve dangerously close to the edge. I feel like I've entered into the presence of a great power. Other people in the car may not feel it at all; they just feel scared.

Feeling like you are being intensely watched in a certain glade or clearing, beside a brook or waterfall, or standing alone in a great expanse of desert is a fairly reliable way of knowing that you are in one of the thin places where the presence of the spirits is particularly strong. But there are other ways to recognize sacred sites. There are no absolutes, however; every place has its own local spirits, and different people are attuned to different manifestations of spirit activity.

Here are some phenomena that have been recorded consistently in sacred sites and places where the earth energies are particularly evident.

> • *Expansion of auras:* Many people experience a kind of expansion of their aura in a sacred site. They feel bigger, more embracing, as well as embraced by some presence that is large and persistent.

• *Mental calm:* Usually our frantic, mental raciness slows down; we stop fretting over things; our roof brain chatter subsides. In fact, right-brain activity often takes an ascendancy, and we perceive colors, shapes, relationships, juxtapositions, and overall patterns.

• *Feelings of unity:* Another indication of being in a sacred site is the ecstatic feeling of being one with something larger than ourselves: unity with the Cosmos or the Creator. Invariably this is experienced as a feeling of awe, joy, or rightfulness with everything in its place, and we begin to think "all's right with the world."

• *Interspecies communication:* It is not uncommon in a power spot to find yourself able to communicate with other species. The wind in the trees has messages. Water falling over stones sounds like words that make sense. We know what the birds are singing about, and we know if their singing is about us or to us.

• *Physical transparency:* The total landscape or some nook within it may become diaphanous, transparent, purer, and permeable so that we begin to see the invisible worlds of color and form on the other side. The cosmic energy or divine power of the universe pours through trees and rocks; a heavenly light illuminates everything and seems to come from within everything.

• *Transcendence and immanence:* There can also be a paradoxical sensation in power spots that the experience you are having is at once transcendent and immanent. We feel transported up and beyond the present moment and place, connected to the greater universe around us, while simultaneously experiencing the power of that greater universe condensed at our very feet, in the air that we breathe, in the colors of the sky that seem to be inside our heads as well as overhead. We transcend time and place, even as all time and all place appear to be contained right where we are. Epiphanies of the sacred intoxicate us with the great mystery and paradox of transcendence and immanence: Creation feels bigger than we ever imagined, while the Creator seems to fit in the hollow of our hand.

• *Loss of sense of self:* Sacred sites have the ability to absorb us as they intoxicate us. We feel drawn into them, desiring to mingle and become one with them, to evaporate and disappear into them. Or failing that, we want to carry home the feeling of headiness or ecstasy that they cause in us and keep it with us throughout life.

Anthropologist and environmentalist James A. Swan has categorized the different types of sacred sites that he has encountered over the years while talking and traveling with Native Americans.[2] We might consider these categories in terms of what they could contribute to our shamanic practice. They include:

• burial grounds and sites

• purification and healing sites where people bathe in sacred waters, fast, meditate, perform ceremonies

• special flora and fauna sites that contain special herbs and animals

• quarries where special stones or gems are found

• vision questing and dreaming sites

• mythic/legendary sites

• temples and shrines where human building enhances the sacredness of the place

• spiritual renewal sites used for pilgrimage or vision quests

• historical sites meaningful to a particular people

• sunrise sites to honor the rising sun at important turning points of the year

- fertility sites

- baptismal sites for bathing and honoring newborn children

Knowing what a site is to be used for is part of the traditional lore and wisdom of indigenous people. In some cases, a place has been used for a certain activity since time immemorial. Clearly as shamanic practitioners, we cannot always find sacred sites that are rich in history and tribal use. Nor would we necessarily want to since we are not part of the tradition that honors and uses the site. In fact, we might be trespassing and dishonoring a site by using it in ways contrary to the native people who have first claim to it. On the other hand, there are some places where no one has first or best claim. Here we should make every effort to know what the place was traditionally used for and conduct ourselves accordingly, either using it in the same or similar manner, or making certain that our own activities do not interfere with or desecrate the primary purpose of the place.

For example, it would do no harm to conduct a night vigil or vision quest on a mountain traditionally used for that, provided our presence did not interfere with native activities. On the other hand, we would not want to trespass on sacred burial grounds by holding a sunrise ritual there. A river or spring with healing properties that is not privately owned should theoretically be available to anyone who would use it respectfully and properly.

Most likely, as shamanic practitioners we will find our own power spots or create our own by intentionally dedicating them in sacred and meaningful ways. What kinds of places could we find or consecrate as sacred? Any place that has played a significant, spiritual, or transformative role in your life is already a sacred site for you, or at least has the potential of becoming one. If you have no such place, then you'll have to discover one. How do you go about it?

In general, look for a place that lures you by its physical beauty or some spectacular feature, a place where you sense the Earth energies are particularly strong. You will probably experience some of the physical, mental, or emotional sensations described above. It will also feel spiritually right for you. What is important is that you *give* the place authority to affect your spiritual life. You formally declare that you will hold the place as sacred and, while there, conduct yourself in a sacred manner. In effect, you create a contract or covenant between yourself and the place. You may not know at first just what type of activity you will carry out there or how often. What matters is a feeling of compatibility and acceptance on both your part and the spirit of the place. If you feel watched, sit down and express your intentions to the spirit there, and begin to see if it and you would benefit from a mutual relationship based on a sacred trust to honor one another's role in the evolving universe. Journey to the spirit of the place or communicate with it, and begin to explore what type of sacred activity you are invited to perform there.

DEVELOPING A SACRED SITE

It is a human urge, and can even be a sacred urge, to leave one's mark on a place. The Celtic tribes were fond of carving faces into tree trunks or stumps, honoring the spirit of the tree or place. Paleolithic artists left spectacular artwork in caves in southern France and northern Spain, painting directly on the walls, and sometimes using the natural features of the wall—bulges, crevices, cracks, and smooth areas—to depict an animal in bas-relief. Stonework left as giant rings in western Europe, Ireland, and Great Britain, as well as the medicine wheels constructed by Native Americans, attest to this age-old desire to leave a human imprint on Mother Earth.

Sacred sites provide mystical anchorings for our spiritual practice, places where time and eternity conjoin, physical reminders of the soul work we do there. They are watchful sentinels guarding the places where we encounter the numinous. It is a natural desire to enhance these settings by making them even more fitting for the spiritual activities we engage in while there. Here are some guidelines for developing a sacred place, either on your own land or in wild areas not privately owned. Obviously, you have more leeway to transform your own land than you do state parks or wilderness areas, so the following suggestions should be adapted accordingly, depending on the extent to which you have a "right" to change the physical environment. In some cases you may want to develop a rather elaborate ceremonial site either for your private use or for a drumming group. In other cases, all you may be able to do is to leave a few charms or sacred objects to hold your presence in the area until you can return.

• *Shape of the land:* Begin by recognizing and incorporating the natural shapes and features of the place. These may not always be immediately obvious. Consider the shape of the land, whether it is flat, hilly, mountainous, overgrown with vegetation, a clearing, a cliff ledge. Include the "borrowed" land, that is, what you can see from the site: distant hills or ranges, a lake, a river below the ledge, a large grove of trees.

• *Individual elements:* Note what elements predominate or share the space: water, plants, trees, animals, soil, sand, pebbles, gravel. Notice the elements of fire in the forms of sunlight and shadow and the element of air in the way the wind or breeze moves through the area. In what direction does the wind approach? How much sunlight falls in the area during the times you will probably use it? Scan the horizons for the points of sunrise and sunset; notice which regions of the sky will be visible at night, and so forth.

• *Spirit faces and voices:* Look around for spirit faces and voices. Sit quietly and gaze at all the trees and rocks to see if there are any faces that could be incorporated into the way you set up the area for rituals or ceremonies, or that might help you decide where you will sit and drum. Listen for voices in the wind, in the trees, or in falling water. You may decide to sit or lie near the voices; or if they are too strong, you might want to keep apart from them if they distract your meditating or journeying.

• *The four directions:* Locate the four directions and mark each point in some way, depending upon how noticeably you can leave signs of your presence. On your own land you might place a large stone, build a cairn (a pile or pillar of stones), or plant flowers to mark each of the cardinal points. In public areas it might be best to use smaller stones, or bury sacred objects in each of the four directions. Crystals or precious stones are good for this, but you can also bury talismans or effigies made of wood, clay, or ceramic. Talismans and effigies could represent the allies you met in each direction as described in Chapter Four. You can also mark each point with some object that stands for the four elements: incense or perfume for air in the east; a candle or burnt ashes for fire in the south; a seashell or small bottle of water in the west; a stone or crystal for earth in the north.

• *Votive offerings:* You can leave very personal items, such as jewelry, photographs, and artwork, either above ground or buried. You might journey on all of this and ask your allies in each direction what would be an appropriate offering. Consider also the possibility of making each object buried a true sacrifice to enhance your rootedness in the land. Many tribal people believe strongly that the spirits require us to give away or dedicate offerings of very significant value. These might be objects you have long treasured and are not inclined to part with easily, or they might be jewelry, tools, and expensive items you purchase for the sole purpose of leaving as a sacrifice.

The Celtic tribes often honored the gods in this way, especially the goddesses of springs and wells, where vast amounts of treasure have been found. Coins, weapons, jewelry, tools, and personal gear have been recovered from bogs that were once lakes and ponds. Many of these objects were not scarred or injured in any way that indicates they were ever used; in other words, they were made or bought precisely to be given away to the spirits.

• *The center:* Create the sacred center of your area. It's possible the area is not geometrically circular enough to locate a true center. If so, decide how you will use the area and determine the place where the major activities will take place. This becomes the "magical center" of the area, even if it is off to the side. For example, a clearing in a forest may have a creek running through it somewhat off-center, and you may decide to create a spot to drum or play a flute just at the place where the creek enters the clearing. This place becomes the magical center for your ritual activity, and so you should "set up" the circumference with directional objects and markers around it accordingly if the site lends itself to this.

• *Altars:* Create a central altar or hub for ritual activity. Outdoor altars can be made of stone, wood, or other permanent material; sometimes a large boulder, a fallen log, or a tree stump lends itself naturally to this use. Altars can also be built off to the side, or in one of the four directions that seems most appropriate for the purpose of the altar. For example, a libation altar could be in the west, the direction of water and the setting sun, or in the east if you intend to use the site in the mornings and pour libations to the rising sun. An altar to leave food for the faery folk seems appropriate for the north, the direction of stone, caves, dells, and shadows. In lieu of an altar, you might want to build a firepit ringed with stones for fire ceremonies.

• *The entry:* Given the physical environment, determine whether there should be a formal entryway into the site. This might be the natural path leading to the area (and possibly the only way to get in), or it might be a ritual entry in one of the four directions that you determine will be the place you officially enter the area for ceremonial work. Some people like to enter through the eastern direction since that is the place the sun enters the sky each morning. The west is also an appropriate entry for evening or night activities. There may be some feature that suggests a ritual entry, such as two trees growing a few feet apart, a gap between two boulders, or the naturally occurring stepping stones that cross a creek. If there is no natural doorway, create an entry with two stones or cairns, or construct an archway or bower with saplings.

• *Ritual tools:* If appropriate, you can leave certain ritual items at the site, such as an incense burner, candles, bowls, cups, cauldrons, a rattle, other ritual tools, and so forth. You can use a small cabinet or box to store these in and protect them from damage.

• *Hermitages:* In many tribal cultures shamans have special huts or cottages for their spiritual and healing work. In the European Christian tradition the woodland hermitage played a similar role for the monk, nun, or hermit who sought to live and pray away from society. You could fix up an old shed for this purpose, or buy a prefabricated shed. If you don't have room on your property outside, a large closet or area of the attic or basement might be suitable. However you prepare it, the place will become a sanctuary for drumming, meditating, or just retiring from the normal day's activities to rest and pray.

When you have constructed your sanctuary or ritual site, dedicate it formally with an appropriate ceremony or gathering of people who participate in your shamanic practice, or by yourself if your shamanic practice is solitary. An all-night drumming session with chanting and dancing is a powerful way to inaugurate a sacred site, beginning at sunset and continuing until dawn. A simpler method is to gather your drumming group and let everyone journey to the spirits to celebrate the place in nonordinary reality, possibly asking for a dance, song, poem, or ritual to bring back and share with the group. Another option is to let everyone journey for a name for the site and then share the names to decide which name it will be, or perform a divination on the names to see which one the spirits select. Then ceremonially bless the area with its sacred name.

THE STORIES OF A PLACE

In many native cultures, certain geographic sites have stories attached to them, sacred stories that become the supernatural archives of a place. In Australia, for example, the Creative Spirits of the land sang the natural features of the landscape into existence. Aborigines still keep the songs and stories of creation alive by walking the land and retelling the tales that came from the Dreamtime when the world was created. Each place has a protective animal spirit connected with it, and according to some traditions, people born in those places receive the spirit animal as a totem that will remain with them for life.

In Ireland the *dindsenchas* are the Gaelic "songlines," stories and tales that connect physical places with the creative powers of the Otherworld—often deities who are the guardian spirits of these places and the bestowers of power, blessings, and grace upon supplicants who make pilgrimage there. For example, the Irish goddess Tailtu was the daughter of the God of the Otherworld, known as the "Great Plain." According to legend, she cleared the land of Ireland and made it arable so that crops would grow, and in so doing exhausted herself, causing her death. Her foster son was the sun god Lugh, and as a tribute to her, he instituted the summer festival of Lughnasad to occur over the two weeks before August 1 and the two weeks following it. During this time great fairs, horse-racing events, and athletic contests of all type take place. Marriages are arranged, and a man and woman who want a trial marriage for a year begin at that time. The area around present-day Telltown is the place where the Lughnasad events occurred.

In tribal cultures the physical landscape is dotted with sacred sites and features imbued with power from the Otherworld. The people traditionally understood the relationship between specific places and their counterparts in the spirit world through stories, mythic descriptions, and ancient songs that clearly expressed the webbed lines of meaning extending from the physical features of the land to the corresponding spirit features in the Otherworld. To walk through the forest or meadow or over a hill was to travel over holy ground.

As modern men and women we often lack this kind of intimate relationship with the land we live on. Modern culture does not preserve or pass on the old stories, and when it does we tend to dismiss them as superstitious, if we understand them at all. But more than likely we find them filled with obscure references to people, events, and "mythical" characters that have no meaning for us. As practitioners of core shamanism we find ourselves preserving and adapting an ancient form of spirituality, but without the physical, earthy setting rich in sacred meanings that could nurture our practice. Shamanism is not just a mental activity, but a physical practice that should be solidly rooted in landscapes that contain sacred histories.

We can, of course, make the study of old stories and legends told by the indigenous peoples of our area part of our academic practice. There is value in knowing and honoring these stories, in being able to recall the tales told about specific mountains, rivers, lakes, or valleys whenever we see them or pass near them. But our goal as practitioners of core shamanism is not to indiscriminately adopt the spiritual traditions of other peoples; nor are we always able to incorporate the characters and events of their stories into our practice, even though knowing those stories enriches our ability to live intelligently and spiritually on the land.

If, for example, you live in Australia, you may naturally wish to weave into your shamanic practice the landforms that you see in the course of your daily life, and you may know some of the dreamsongs told by the Aborigines. The cosmic and natural forces that created the landscape—underground rivers, storms, earth upheavals, and so forth—are the creative Ancestors who imbued the land with the life force that has allowed the people to live there happily for more than 100,000 years. The stories of these Ancestors, retold from generation to generation, may be inspiring to you, but attempting to incorporate them into your spiritual practice might ring somewhat hollow and inauthentic because you are not part of the indigenous people of the land.

Not being able to fully utilize (or even understand) the local native stories of the Original Time presents us with a difficult paradox because we want to work with the spirits of place, but the shapes, forms, stories, and associations concerning those spirits speak of another people's ancient bonds of kinship with the land, not our own. The tales may not hold the numinous qualities we need to make them relevant to our spiritual practices. So we may need to ask the spirits to tell us new stories and new songlines more suited to the unique struggles we live through as we strive to find the numinous in contemporary life. The spirits of place are not restricted to the old stories; they can adapt the older tales to the current age and to current seekers.

A journey to discover the new stories begins with asking your power animal to take you to the spirit of a place important to you in your current life and for which you would like to know the spirit story that will hold meaning for you. It may be good to ask for the story in pieces so that you can assimilate them slowly, allowing the full story to grow into consciousness at a pace that reveals its meanings and relevance to you in a measured way. Receiving a full-blown story might impact upon us like the full-blown stories we are continually bombarded with on television and in the movies—in one ear, out the other. The sacred stories of indigenous people were learned slowly, sometimes part by part, as a process of initiation over the years from childhood to adulthood. The stories revealed their secrets piece by piece.

One way to begin the process of learning your stories a little at a time is to ask the spirit of a place the following questions:

- Have you been with me earlier in this life?

- In what form did you/your power appear or manifest to me then?

- What have I forgotten about you over the years since then?

- Do you continue to influence me in some other form or shape that I don't recognize as being you?

With these questions you will become acquainted with the spirit of a place in terms of your own life history, and you can gradually allow the full story to take form and meaning, honoring various aspects of it so that they become fully integrated into your consciousness. When they become second nature to you, you will recognize them as being truly and authentically part of your spiritual journey and not something tacked on from another people's traditions.

Let's take an example. You live near a small mountain with a ledge jutting out over a river. You have lived here for several years. You want to meet the spirit of this place—the Ledge Spirit—because you go there to drum or meditate; and you would like to know the story of the area. There are old legends about the ledge as a site where Native Americans did vision quests in earlier times before the tribe was forced to leave the area, and there are pioneer stories about the place being a lover's leap. You know specific, detailed stories from both traditions, but none suit your current shamanic practice. Clearly the ledge has a strong imprint of earlier human experiences, and clearly the Ledge Spirit draws you to it.

If you approach the Ledge Spirit with questions similar to the ones suggested above, you might be told information something like this: Yes, the Spirit of the Ledge is the same kind of spirit power as that of the Riverbank where you went to study and make plans about your future life when you were in college. What you have forgotten about the Spirit is that it is a source of strength and courage for planning important changes in your life. The Ledge Spirit might point out that the spirit of your deceased grandmother, who occasionally meets you in shamanic journeys and communicates with you during reflective moments, is filling the same need in your life as the Spirits of the Riverbank and the Ledge. She offers you counsel similar to the advice she gave you while she was alive. In other words, Riverbank, Grandmother, and Ledge are a trio of spirits who play similar roles in your life. Knowing this, the ledge itself—the physical spot over the river—becomes part of your earlier life, your family, and your current life situation. Its story begins to take shape as part of your personal mythology.

Deepen your journeys and meditations so that this story becomes solidly interwoven into your past and present life and the life of the ledge over the river. At some point, ask the Ledge Spirit's name, and ask it to tell you other stories about what has happened in the area or about incidents that involved it, and to teach you how to become more spiritually connected to the place. In time, a story will emerge that is personal, comforting, and empowering, a story that becomes part of the sacred archives that contain your life. It may turn out that the story that emerges, both from the spirit's tellings and your contemplation on the details, will incorporate some of the elements of the Native American stories and the pioneer legends that are relevant to your own practice. Or perhaps none of the older history proves meaningful for you, and the story of the place is truly a unique, private songline known only by you and the spirit of the place.

LEY LINES, TRACKWAYS, AND FAERY PATHS

There is a universal sense that the Earth is webbed with life forces and energies that influence human activity, especially the laying out of roadways and construction of sacred buildings. In the Western world, the modern interest in this kind of webbing began in 1921 when Alfred Watkins noticed a line stretching across the English countryside, connecting churches, wells, castles, standing stones, and other markers indicating that human beings have taken a more-than-coincidental interest in utilizing this invisible path. He called this path of natural and human artifacts "the Old Straight Track." Eventually called "ley lines," such courses of energy have inspired scientists, metaphysicians, spiritualists, dowsers, and folklorists to delve into their deeper meanings. Similar lines or tracks have been discovered on other continents, often coinciding with Neolithic structures, suggesting that our ancestors everywhere recognized the earth forces normally imperceptible to the human senses, and that these became the grid upon which people expressed some of their strongest spiritual aspirations.

Similar concepts of energy lines are found in China in the art of *feng shui*, the ancient practice of using the natural energies of a place as a kind of spiritual blueprint for building and land use. In Ireland similar earth forces are known as faery paths and are still taken seriously by some builders. If you build a house on a faery path, you disrupt the faeries' accustomed travel routes, and they may take revenge by causing bad luck or making the house itself weaken and crumble. A traditional way to test for a faery path before you start to build is to turn over four pieces of sod where the four corners of the house will sit and leave them there for two or three days. If one of them has been turned back over when you return, the faeries have given warning. It would be best to move your location or redesign the house so that it does not sit over the faery path.

Human beings are naturally attracted to ley lines and faery places because the energies of the Earth are exceptionally strong there; they are natural power spots where we feel our senses peaked and our conscious awareness lightened and raised. To varying degrees, a sense of well-being pervades us physically, mentally, emotionally, and spiritually; it feels good to be there. And in general it is, unless your purpose for using the spot is not in harmony with the local spirits. As shamanic practitioners we should know and live in sync with the natural energy lines that cross our land.

The most common way of discovering energy lines is by dowsing with a rod or a pendulum. Books on dowsing and ley lines can provide information on how to go about it. However, there is a shamanic way of discovering the natural currents of energy in your area that might be equally, if not more, useful to you. Plan a journey with your power animal to see the lines of force, the webbing of spiritual energy that undergirds the terrain around your home. If you want to know the actual physical features of the land that you will see from a spiritual perspective on the shamanic journey, study a topographic map before you journey to familiarize yourself with the major land features in the area. Look for the tallest hills or mountains, major rivers, streams, and lakes, the shape of the coastline, important changes in elevation, various valleys. Note the directions these ranges, rivers, and valleys run. It is not necessary to commit the map to memory or know the exact elevations. Rather you are simply trying to get a preview of what the area will look like from above.

Then do a middle-world journey that incorporates the following activities.

1. Ascend or fly with your power animal above the area.

2. Ask the spirits to let you see the energy currents, ley lines, and faery paths that course through and run along the natural features.

3. Also ask to see the spirit patterns, which may or may not coincide with the physical terrain. These might be spirals, webs, waves, domes, or circular constructions with a three-dimensional component. These energy lines and patterns may appear in different colors or textures.

4. Either on the journey or later, perhaps on a hike through part of the landscape, ask to be taught what the energy of different locations is for, how to live in harmony with these energies, and how to use them (if possible) to help maintain environmental balance. In other words, as a member of the biotic and geologic communities in the area, find out how you can promote the ecological health of the area on both a physical and spiritual level.

5. Find out what your stewardship of the land requires. You may learn that the land spirits would like you to perform specific rituals in, or for, certain areas at various times of the year, such as the solstices and equinoxes.

PILGRIMAGE, NIGHT VIGIL, AND VISION QUEST

There is an old story told about a proper English anthropologist who was traveling through a distant land interviewing and studying native people. One night while camped between villages, he heard drumming deep in the woods. Intrigued, he set down his cup of tea and headed in the direction of the drum. He came upon a clearing where a man was drumming and dancing around a fire. The man chanted and sang, put down the drum, picked up rattles, and continued his ecstatic movements around the fire. After about an hour of continuous dancing, drumming, and rattling, the man sat down to rest. The anthropologist approached and said politely, "Sir, I have been admiring your ritual. You must tell me what it's all about. Why are you here all alone, dancing, drumming, rattling, chanting? What does it all mean?" The native looked at him, puzzled, and asked, "What do you mean 'all alone'?"

Back to square one for the Englishman, who lacked the perspective of indigenous people, such as the Dakota Sioux, who teach their children that there is no such thing as complete solitude. Wherever we go we are surrounded by life—conscious, responsive, and communicative. Spiritual activity even in the apparently isolated wilds of nature is never truly "alone," for the so-called wilderness is densely peopled with spirits. By spending time "alone with the spirits" a shaman receives wisdom. Igjugarjuk, an Eskimo/Caribou shaman, put it this way:

> True wisdom is only to be found far away from people, out in the great solitude, and it is not found in play but only through suffering. Solitude and suffering open the human mind, and therefore a shaman must seek his wisdom there.[3]

Part of our spiritual practice should be to spend periods of time in the solitude of nature. We each need this, especially people who live in congested and heavily populated urban environments, but even practitioners living in the country will need to get away from their usual routines, family, and friends to be alone with the spirits. There are three ways to seek this wisdom-time: pilgrimages, night vigils, and vision quests.

PILGRIMAGE

I use the word *pilgrimage* intentionally to indicate the sacred nature of this kind of activity. Historically pilgrimages involved travel to destinations considered holy, either as officially constructed places important to an organized religion, such as temples, churches, and shrines, or as natural settings that a religious tradition holds important for some special reason. Natural destinations, such as springs or wells, might be places where miraculous healings occur, or a place where some important event transpired in the history of that religion, such as the site where its founder or one of its leaders received enlightenment or perhaps died.

For the shamanic practitioner the pilgrimage to a sacred place in nature can be as easy as a few hours' hike to a waterfall or grove of trees where you have ongoing relationships with the spirits or where you go to perform simple rituals. We should not dismiss the one-day hike as a form of spiritual practice. Even a hike along an unfamiliar woodland trail or through a state park you have never yet explored can be done in the spirit of pilgrimage, to spend time closer to nature than you ordinarily do in your daily life, to seek instruction and wisdom from the spirits of that place or from your own spirits who accompany you on the trek.

As a body practice, hiking, camping, rock climbing, or canoeing gets us outside into the natural world. We show the spirits by our physical exertion that we take our practice seriously, and the "little" sufferings that may occur along the way—fatigue, thirst, sweat, blisters, scratches, and bites—are signs of our commitment to know nature and the forces of nature in a bodily way. As Igjugarjuk says, it is through suffering that wisdom comes.

NIGHT VIGIL

The night vigil has a long and honored place in spiritual practices: spending the night awake in a prayerful attitude in a chapel, sanctuary, graveyard, or even one's home. Even if the mind cannot stay focused on prayer all night, the physical act of keeping watch through the midnight hours is spiritually worthwhile. As shamanic practitioners we can undertake a night vigil at home or in a place outdoors we consider to be a sacred site. Indeed, spending a night awake, praying or drumming in a power spot, is an ideal way to bless the site and make it your own.

You might want to fast the day before a vigil, consuming only liquids until you break your fast the next morning. Arrive at the site sometime before sunset, preferably early in the day to take full advantage of being there. Collect firewood if you intend to have a fire, although you might not want to have to fiddle with it, preferring instead to free your spirit and attention for your night watch. On the other hand, the company of fire spirits can be comforting and instructive.

Commit yourself to staying awake from sunset to sunrise. If you do fall asleep, do not be too self-critical or consider the vigil a failure. Not everyone can stay awake the full night, and it's quite possible the spirits will fill your sleep with dreams to teach and empower you. Falling asleep is also a teaching about our weakness, our bodily needs, our need to try again. No effort is wasted if the intentions are pure.

VISION QUEST

A vision quest is a longer stay, often three to four days, in the solitary places of nature. In some cultures the vision quester, fasting and naked, remains awake in a seated position and may perform simple rituals and say certain prayers, beseeching the spirits to send a powerful vision that will transform his or her life. As part of your academic practice you might read up on vision quest customs in different societies. Keep in mind that you do not have to adopt any culture's complete practice and carry it out in the same way. In the spirit of core shamanism, learn the various ways a vision quest can be done, and select the features that appeal to you. Journey on this and ask your helping spirits how to plan a vision quest that suits your purposes. There is no one right way to seek a vision. A sleeping bag can substitute for a blanket, a bottle of water can be taken for drinking, insect repellent can be used. It is up to you and your spirit instructors to decide what should and should not be taken along, keeping in mind that we all come to this practice with different needs and expectations. We are also at different levels of spiritual and physical development, so what is right for one person may not be for someone else, and vice versa.

In general, however, you want to leave as much "stuff" behind as possible: reading materials, journal and pen, audio tapes, clothing and other supplies that are crutches—the things we think we can't live without. One of the goals of the vision quest is to teach us that we can survive without our security blankets. For many people whose spiritual practice involves ritual items, it can be very difficult leaving even them at home. A favorite crystal, rattle, incense, even a drum might be a spiritual crutch that interferes with our goals of solitude and hardship, which we hope will lead us to wisdom. Each individual must decide the extent of the deprivations and suffering he or she plans to endure, remembering that there will always be other vision quests in the future to increase the intensity.

As mentioned earlier, if you plan to stay out in nature for any length of time, even for a one-night vigil, alert others as to your whereabouts and when they can expect you to return. Also, as far as possible, check to see that the place you have chosen is safe. Riverbeds can be subject to flash floods; in some regions, temperatures drop rapidly after sunset; some areas may be dangerous because of wild animals; unsavory characters prowl some parks and trails looking for someone to rob or harass.

Shamanism as a spiritual practice should instill in us strong ecological perceptions that reveal how intricately nature and human life are interconnected. The spiritual life of nature is not separate from our own. In fact, we might argue from a shamanic point of view that our spiritual lives emerge *from and out* of the natural forces of the Earth. Our practice, insofar as it returns us to the wild and free places in nature, reaffirms this perception and deepens it. Then, even though we are relative newcomers, living on lands that are not indigenous to our bloodline ancestors, we can begin to make commitments to the spirits of the places where we live and to create covenants based on the ethics of mutual respect and assistance.

CHAPTER SEVEN

THE SECRETS OF CHILDHOOD

I remember the first time I heard someone answer the question, "How did you get involved in shamanism?" It was at a weekend workshop in the mid-1980s, and the woman being asked answered, "Well, I read a book on shamanism about eight years ago and started hanging out with Native Americans." The questioner smiled and nodded, seemingly satisfied with the answer, but the woman continued almost without taking a breath. "But you know, when I was a kid, I knew there were spirits in the woods and I had a favorite spot back in there by a creek where I would go to talk to them." On hearing this, I had a rush of *déjà vu*: I could have given the same answer.

Since then I have noticed repeatedly that most people when asked about their introduction to shamanism give a two-part answer. First, they will say that they "met a shaman" or "participated in a shamanic training program" or "read a book on shamanism" five, eight, or ten years ago. Then they will offer a second piece of information that is even more revealing of their spiritual search. They will say something to the effect of: "But when I was a kid, I used to see elves in the backyard" or "When I went on picnics with my family in the state parks, I talked to the ghosts in the woods" or "When I listened to the church choir chant in Latin, I would go into altered states of consciousness and have visions of saints and angels." Many admit that they had invisible friends or guardian angels with whom they had complex, ongoing relationships.

Shamanic practitioners instinctively recognize parallels between their shamanic practice and childhood experiences. Ironically these same individuals often feel disadvantaged as shamanic practitioners because they have not been born into and raised in indigenous cultures that live in intimate relationships with the land, animals, and the spirits of nature. The "wannabe" syndrome can be powerful. And they have a point. Children raised in cultural environments where people appreciate and honor the spiritual dimensions of nature find the encouragement and support from parents to develop the natural mysticism of childhood. Americo Yabar, a shaman of the Q'ero people who live in the Andes of south-central Peru, explains this.

> Just living in the mountains gives a child spiritual advantage. From birth, the child is near the fire and is underneath the stars. The child relates to the alpaca and the puma. The child speaks with the stones, speaks with the plants in a very natural way. In the mountains, magical interactions with the elements occur on a daily basis. So even children know with certainty that their world is populated by spirits—the river has a spirit, the tree has a spirit, the stone has a spirit.[1]

The Q'ero child's experiences are typical of children everywhere, regardless of environment. Children spontaneously communicate with animals, birds, flowers, and toys. Unfortunately in most modern cultures, these activities do not survive into adulthood, but the memory of these experiences does survive on some unconscious level and surfaces into awareness when people are introduced to shamanism for the first time. They are startled to realize that they have done this kind of thing before.

A similar experience occurred to Kai Donner, who visited the Samoyed people in Siberia in the early twentieth century. Sitting with some of the tribal people around a fire, Donner listened to old men tell ancient legends and shamans report on their journeys to the upper and lower worlds.

I suddenly felt like a child and, as in childhood, I imagined that every object had its spirit, that water and air were populated by mysterious invisible beings who, in inexplicable fashion, ruled the course of the world and the fate of men. In the untouched wilderness and its infinite silence, I was encompassed by the traditional mysticism and religious mysteries through which faith touches so many things.[2]

The traditional mysticism and religious mysteries of which Donner speaks are characteristic of childhood, and the spontaneously retrieved childhood memories of people discovering shamanic practices later in life reflect the persistence of that mysticism. Our innate mysticism, which seems to fade during the long, arduous route to adulthood, is never totally quenched. The simplest activity—sitting on the floor in a circle around a candle, shaking a rattle in a semi-darkened room, listening to the ancient sound of a drum resonating with the intimate beating of our heart—can reawaken the thoughts and feelings of the child-shaman-mystic hiding deep within us.

We do not "discover" shamanism late in life, totally bereft of any previous shamanic experience. Our first mystical insights and spiritual discoveries occurred when we were quite young, and we can tap into those visionary adventures for the shamanic lore they can provide us in our current practice of core shamanism. In this chapter we will look at the natural shamanism of children, along with the strong societal and cultural forces operating against it, and we will explore methods for reawakening and recapturing the spirit and secrets of our own childhood that provided our first shamanic experiences.

THE CREATION OF CHILDHOOD AS A STAGE OF LIFE

Childhood as we know it did not exist in the Western world until around 1600. In researching family life in western Europe, social historians discovered that around 1600, middle-class children began embarking on a pattern of training—indeed, a pattern of life—that by the nineteenth century would be extended to the children of lower- and working-class families. Today, in the twentieth century, we uncritically assume that every boy or girl should traverse this same path from birth to adulthood, which can last until a young person is well into his or her twenties. In other words, Western society created "stages of life" called "childhood" and "adolescence" in which the natural mysticism of children would be systematically replaced by a linear, rational, scientific way of perceiving reality, which would make earlier childlike perceptions appear to be "fantasy" and "make-believe."

Considerable evidence suggests that childhood was not a "stage of life" until around 1600, when the Industrial-Protestant-Scientific Revolutions occurred in Western thought and culture (the date is somewhat arbitrary since obviously something like a stage of life could not be created and imposed in any one given year). Prior to the seventeenth century, children and adults shared the same world and lived in the same physical and psychic environments. Children were not separated from adult experiences and segregated into environments composed primarily of children their own age whose experiences were not shared by adults.

For example, adults and children wore the same style clothes, played the same kinds of games, participated in the same storytelling events, ate the same food, slept in the same room (often in the same bed), and engaged in the same work activities. The "toys" children played with were miniature versions of the tools that adults used or the tools themselves. When adults and children were segregated in activities or tasks, it was due to the disparity in physical size and strength. A child would be given only those chores he or she was physically capable of performing. Children might play together for the same reasons—they were more equal physically—but they played the same kinds of games as adults.

The folk tales collected by the Grimm brothers and others in the nineteenth century today seem alarmingly violent, cruel, and obscene. They relate graphic descriptions of incest, sadistic parents and step-parents, self-mutilation, maimings, devourings by wild beasts, and revenge—themes that our modern sensibilities deem inappropriate for children. But we need to remember that these were not children's stories originally. They were just stories that all ages listened to and enjoyed. Only when childhood became a stage of life, and folk and fairy tales were considered to be the domain of children, did these stories seem somehow wrong for children and in need of sanitizing.

When children lived on intimate terms with adults, they did not remain ignorant of the facts of life: sex, birth, death, and the need to take life. Children witnessed these events routinely, either among animals or among the adults with whom they lived. The notion that children are "innocent" and need "protection" from these realities is part of the modern sensibility that emerged around 1600.

In village and tribal cultures, children and adults live intimately with each other. Children learn how to become adults by imitating their parents and other adults—similar, of course, to how the offspring of all species develop into maturity. They watch, imitate, and strive to do what the elders do. What may seem remarkable to us in the twentieth century is that children in indigenous cultures *want* to become adults, and want to be *like* adults. Furthermore, tribal children do not, in general, fear adults, run away when adults are present, or show fear around strangers. It makes sense that the life force, bent on survival, would provide the young of all species with a natural desire to imitate elders in order to ensure a natural growth into adulthood.

Jean Liedloff, who lived among the Yequana tribe in Venezuela and documented the relationship between adults and children in her classic book *The Continuum Concept*, noted that six- and seven-year-old boys and girls routinely paddled canoes without the supervision of adults in some of the most treacherous white-water rapids in the world. By that age they had not only learned canoeing skills by being in canoes from birth, watching adults canoe, and handling paddles themselves under adult supervision when they were strong enough, but what is even more remarkable, they had learned responsibility. They could accept a task without complaint, even without the bickering between the sexes that we think is natural to young children asked to help each other in the same project.³

Why did this more natural way of raising children not survive in the West?

The need for a highly educated populace that emerged with the development of urban life at the time of the Industrial Revolution produced the graded school system that has come to dominate childhood and adolescence in the modern world. The ability to read, write, and perform mathematical tasks, and a comprehensive knowledge of the extended world around us (science, history, literature, art, etc.), became necessities for the evolving lifestyle of western Europe. Today the basic skills and knowledge needed to survive and participate successfully in our society require not only grammar and high school, but college and post-graduate studies and training. We have postponed adulthood and the responsibilities of adulthood well beyond the age of puberty when a boy or girl becomes physically a young man or woman. Many young people today postpone their full entry into adulthood—career or full-time job, marriage, beginning a family of their own—until they are in their early or middle twenties, or even later, a good ten to fifteen years after puberty. In brief, a person spends one-fourth to one-third of his or her life preparing to become an adult. This is not what nature originally intended.

The natural mysticism of childhood, or what is often described as the magical, nonrational thinking of childhood, is rigorously suppressed as the child progresses from grade to grade, level to level, learning the left-brain, rational, scientific, technologically oriented way of thinking and acting required for the modern world. This can be seen clearly in children's artwork. Until around age eleven, children draw very shamanically. A house, a bird, a tree, even a little girl's sketch of herself may all be the same size on the page; colors may not correspond to actual colors in nature. The child could care less. To the child's mystical awareness, the drawing makes sense. At age eleven or thereabouts, the child becomes frustrated with drawing and will copy the same sketch over and over, crumpling up each attempt and throwing it on the floor in an effort to draw "realistically," which means photographically or the way it "really looks." In time the child's imaginative, nonordinary perceptions of the world, transposed onto the sketch pad, are embarrassing and childish. And most children (read: most of us!) become convinced we have no talent. We stop drawing.

RECAPTURING THE SPIRIT OF CHILDHOOD

From birth until around age nine, each of us lived through what may have been the most spiritually creative and mystically oriented phase of our lives. In general, parents and adults, almost as if they intuitively realize that these years are precious from a spiritual point of view, encourage this natural mysticism. Children are expected to play, fantasize, daydream, and dream, enjoying the faery lore, make-believe, and spontaneous games that are second nature to us. Or perhaps adults, realizing regretfully that they too gave up this way of being in the world in order to become adults, hope to recapture something of this early life vicariously by encouraging it in their children and reliving it through the eyes of their sons and daughters.

In tribal and village communities, children and adults share the major elements of their lives with each other; a child's activities and experiences more or less reflect those of adults, and vice versa. The physical, psychic, and *spiritual* environments are the same. A child who encounters the Little People in the woods, hears an animal speak to her, or has a dream about the culture's heroes or deities can share these experiences with adults. Somewhere in the village is a grandmother or grandfather who also has encounters with the Little People, speaks with animal spirits, and dreams of the same gods and goddesses. As tribal and village children become more competent in physical tasks and assume adult responsibilities, they do not relinquish the natural spirituality with which they are born. Indeed, there is no need to do so, for they see adults in the community who still view the world in these spiritually connected ways and lead productive lives because of it.

Although our childhood visionary experiences were similar to those of tribal and village children living in less urbanized and technologized societies, we have suffered severe deprivations in terms of support and self-confidence. Most of us did not share our private dreams and so-called fantasies with adults because we knew they did not share them. When we awoke from a nightmare, a parent often calmed us down by telling us "not to be afraid because it wasn't real." We intuitively sensed that adults did not enjoy—or believe in—the fairy tales they read to us as much as we did. I never heard adults sharing with each other vision-ary encounters with the same heroic and mythic beings that peopled my life: Robin Hood, Superman, Peter Pan, Spin and Marty. And most of us were separated from physical contact with adults minutes after birth. We had our own rooms, beds, play areas. We were given toys and games to amuse us that had no counterparts among adults.

For our shamanic practice we should reconnect with the visionary experiences we had as children for several reasons. First, they were our initial mystical experiences and those most natural to us, and they remain influential either consciously or unconsciously as part of our memory bank of life experiences. Second, the personal spirits with whom we had intimate, ongoing relationships might still be playing active roles in our lives today, and it would be helpful to realize how they stayed with us over the years or returned once we began our shamanic practice. Third, one of the goals of any spiritual practice is to prepare us for death by making sense of this life, including the years of childhood and adolescence.

On the day we were born we entered life with a fearless sense of communion with people and nature. We had no concept or fear of death. Henry David Thoreau lamented that he was not as wise as on the day he was born.[4] Black Elk advised that we "learn from very little chil-dren, for the hearts of little children are pure, and therefore, the Great Spirit may show to them many things which older people miss."[5] This is the wisdom that we seek in our shamanic practice.

OUR FIRST SPIRIT ALLIES

Shamans assume that we are always protected and watched over by helping spirits—how could we have survived this long in life if we were not
protected? If this is true, then guardian spirits have cared for us since our
earliest years. Many of us were told as children that we had personal
guardian angels, and some of us developed relationships with them
through prayer and religious devotions. But in addition to the "official"
spirit guardians encouraged by adults and religious leaders, many children acquire other spirit helpers in the forms of invisible friends, elves,
animal companions, and cultural heroes either created by the popular
media—such as the Disney characters—or drawn from older folk traditions—such as the fairy tales collected in earlier centuries.

We must keep in mind that spirits are shapeshifters and will appear
to us in the forms and guises that make sense to us, that we can accept,
that will "work." Spirits do this in every culture. If we reflect for a
moment on the situation in tribal cultures where there is no popular
media churning out new heroes every few years, where adults and children share the same stories and experiences of a finite set of deities,
spirits, and culture heroes, everyone in the community encounters the
spirits in basically the same forms.

But in our culture, where children's experience is radically different
from that of adults, we should expect the spirits to use the forms currently available and appropriate to children's imaginative needs. Donald
Duck, Minnie Mouse, Miss Piggy, Barbie, the Ninja Turtles, Barney,
Big Bird, or whatever cartoon or comic book character is currently playing a major role in children's visionary and dreaming lives can serve as
a vehicle for helping spirits. The characters that we admire, either as
children or adults, tend to resemble each other in that they are manifestations of certain archetypal forms that remain the same throughout
human experience even though their physical shapes change from culture to culture. In this sense, the Green Man of the Forest, Robin Hood,
Daniel Boone, Tarzan, and Huckleberry Finn share archetypal energy,
and a helping spirit can use the popular imagery of these various figures

to appeal to a young child who needs a spirit companion who lives an unfettered life outside the bounds of family and society.

We can see how these childhood heroes or companions played a helping role in our lives when we consider that some of us actually talked to them, carried on complicated conversations, and followed their advice. They comforted us when we were sad, instructed us on how to survive childhood challenges and disappointments, and provided an ear for us when we could not complain to adults who seemed too busy to listen to our chatter. Some of us fantasized about the lives these companions lived, hoping that we would one day grow up to be just like them, imagining that we were these characters and had their strengths, virtues, and adventures.

It may require some suspension of disbelief for us to look back and accept these "childish fantasies" as serious manifestations of spiritual help, but they were. Spirits appear to us in the imaginal realm of our consciousness, which is structured by specific people, places, objects, shapes, and forms whether we are fifty years old or five years old. We have been so brainwashed to devalue childhood experiences as being of little worth to our adult lives that we can easily overlook the important role these childhood companions played in our lives, and may continue to play. For these reasons, we should journey to our former spirit helpers to reconnect and renew that relationship. Here is a way to do this.

1. Sit for a few minutes shaking a rattle, asking your power animal to join you and indicate to you which visionary companion of your childhood is the one to whom you should journey at this time. It's possible you have several in mind, or you might not be able to think of any at the moment. Your power animal will be able to focus your memory.

• Do not choose someone you actually knew as a child, such as a friend's older sister or a dashing uncle, no matter how much you fantasized about them. The point is to make this journey to someone who figured in your life solely as a visionary companion, not a friend or acquaintance in ordinary reality.

• The spirit companion can be in the form of a historical figure, such as Joan of Arc or Daniel Boone, because your knowledge and experience of this person was in the imaginative realm, not ordinary reality.

• A popular animal, such as Lassie, Rin Tin Tin, Simba, the Lion King, or a personal animal companion such as a unicorn or an imaginary crow, can also be used.

• If you and your power animal cannot come up with any figure who played this kind of major helping role in your life, think back over all the fictional or historical characters you simply admired, even though they may not be paragons of heroism. It's possible your recall is faulty or you have repressed your childhood visionary heroes. Journeying to a character you admired can unlock earlier memories, and you may discover other companion spirits by consulting with the admired figure.

2. Ask your power animal to take you to this childhood companion and ask these three questions:

• What have I forgotten about you?

• Do you have any help/power/instruction for my current life situation?

• Do you continue to influence me in some other form or shape?

These questions usually begin to reveal the spiritual links that connect our adult shamanic practice with the spontaneous shamanism of childhood.

The significance of this childhood spirit companion can be seen in the current lives of many shamanic practitioners. They frequently discover that the spirit helper has very relevant advice or power for their current lives, and many spirits say they continue to help us in other forms, sometimes closely related to the original form from childhood. For example, a Robin Hood spirit may continue to function in a person's shamanic practice as a Forest Spirit, perhaps a Green Man or the spirit of a specific grove of trees. The information forgotten about the childhood companion can also be quite revealing in terms of the practitioner's lost idealism or faded adolescent dreams.

To follow up on this, ask yourself if there is any connection between your childhood hero and your current career, lifestyle, or avocation. Often people find the connection very easily. For example, a woman whose childhood spirit helper was Lassie is now a teenage drug counselor, still helping young people out of trouble. A man whose hero was Spiderman is now a professional rock climber and spelunker. A woman who admired Nancy Drew as a girl is a district attorney.

In general, I've discovered that people who find some strong link between their childhood hero and their current life tend to be fairly happy and satisfied. People who see no connection are often dissatisfied or unfulfilled with their current careers or ways of living. This is not a hard and fast rule, but it does point out the important role that the helping spirits from childhood play in our lives, both at an early age by inspiring us with possible career options and by encouraging us along the way to make the choices that will let those dreams come true. If you see no connection and are not pleased with your current life, then perhaps you should embark on a series of journeys to this spirit to explore what is wrong with your current lifestyle and how you might change. The answers to the question, "What have I forgotten about you?" might be the key.

Another issue you may want to explore with your childhood spirit helper is whether it will continue to be part of your spiritual practice, either in its original form or some other form, or whether it no longer has a role to play in your life. Some spirits are with us only for very specific periods of time to assist in specific situations; then they depart. But you can always ask if the spirit has some purpose for your current life, and if so, then begin journeys and rituals to reestablish your relationship.

CHILDREN AND ANIMALS

Children have a natural affinity for animals, and unless they are startled by an animal's unpredicted movement or sound, they have no fear of animals. A young child will drop a stuffed bear and run up to a live bear at the zoo to get close, reaching out to touch it. In this we see how powerful is the life force, the innate drive to merge with some living being other than the Self, to realize the mystical oneness that characterizes life in the womb. Such a fearlessness, however, usually doesn't last long, for parents and other adults teach children to be wary and fearful around strange animals.

Researchers into childhood behavior tell us that from ages four to seven, a child dreams more frequently about animals than humans; and the animals that appear in a child's dreams are not the family cat, dog, or parakeet. They are wild animals, barnyard animals, animals seen in the zoo or on television, animals that represent a dramatic "other" quality to the child's life, that live in a nonordinary reality compared to the child's. It has been suggested that children are naturally attracted to animals because, unlike adults, an animal is unambiguous, direct, forthright, honest. Animals do not lie, deceive, cheat, keep secrets. If they growl, they growl. If they run toward you, they really come. If they back off, they are wary of you. They don't dissemble. A child can "read" animals (with practice) and be assured that animals mean exactly what they appear to mean.

Perhaps this is why we felt so at ease with invisible animal companions. We "pretended" they were with us or that we were those animals, imagining we were horses or deer as we ran across the grass; we shapeshifted into them in consciousness. As animals, we did not have to play the ambiguous games of adults or live up to their uncertain expectations of us. We knew who we were, we knew what to do. We did it.

Children love stories about animals and seem to need representations of them around: pictures on the bedroom walls; prints on sheets and blankets; soft stuffed animals; animals made out of ceramic, clay, or carved from wood. Cartoons and comics about animals, with either realistic or stylized drawings, stir something deep and important in the child's imagination. An animated movie of animals is hard to resist. As the child grows, we use stories about anthropomorphic animals to teach lessons about, ironically, how to be a human being! We discover the faults and follies of human behavior in stories about human-like animals. Animals are among our first teachers.

Because the Self is not rigid in childhood, because the ego boundaries are still fluid, it is easy for children to take on the characteristics of animals and move and act like them, imagining that they can be animals whenever they want. In shamanic terms, children are natural shapeshifters. They find great consolation in merging with animal spirits, for such experiences allow the child to leave ordinary reality—the reality of parents and adults where the rules are confusing and difficult—and spend time in the nonordinary realms of the spirit world.

I remember a girl who could run faster than anyone in our neighborhood. We called her Gator. Gator used to say that she wished she had been born a horse. She not only won every race, but she ran wherever she went: school, the corner store, over to friends' houses. She despised bikes. One summer, word went around that Gator ate purple clover in the vacant lots around the neighborhood, and soon we were all furtively chomping on purple clover in the parks and cemeteries, hoping this was the secret of Gator's swiftness. It seemed to make sense: horses ate clover; horses ran fast. Gator was part horse. You are what you eat. Somehow my father got wind of this, or smelled the clover on my breath (as a few years later he would smell cigarette smoke), and took a dim view of it. He talked me out of munching on weeds, and so I resigned myself to never being able to keep up with Gator. Other kids gave up too: both grazing on purple clover and trying to outrun her. Today Gator raises horses in the Midwest.

Around age seven, animal dreams decline, and children begin to dream more consistently of their parents, teachers, siblings, and friends. Stories in which a human is turned into an animal take on a fearsome quality, as the child's developing ego boundaries reinforce the notion that the child is a separate self, distinct from other creatures. A child's task is to become civilized, learn the rules, develop social manners. The dichotomy of "tame versus wild" begins to have a meaning for the child that will probably persist throughout life, eventually growing into the overly civilized fear of any life that is too organic, dirty, untamed, wild. The child will eventually learn not to play in mud, enjoy bugs, pick its nose in public, and talk about excrement with such great delight.

As shamanic practitioners we have already reconnected with the spirits of organic life—animals, soil, elements, plants—and in so doing we re-create that oneness with the cosmos that was spontaneous, natural, and total in our earliest years. But we can do more. Here are some goals for journeying to the spirit of a particular animal companion or fantasy animal that you had as a child.

- Hang out and play with it, just as you may have done as a child.

- Shapeshift into it and re-experience the power and attributes of that animal.

- Ask if it will continue to play a role as a spirit advisor or companion in your shamanic practice.

- Ask for advice on how to handle your own children.

When doing soul retrievals, I often ask for a power animal to accompany an aspect of the soul that left in early childhood, and I've been surprised how often the power animal turns out to be a young animal: a fawn, a baby wolf or fox, a young zebra. Occasionally I will do a power animal retrieval for someone and ask specifically for an immature power animal, if this type of youthful energy would be advantageous for the person's situation. You might consider whether a young animal spirit would bring a new quality to your own spiritual life, and if so, journey to find one. It might become an ally in other journeys and rituals to reconnect with the spirit of childhood and reclaim the natural mysticism you once knew as a child.

REVISITING EARLY POWER SPOTS

In Chapter Six we considered the importance of having the spirits of places as spiritual instructors. Now in our effort to recapture the spiritual experiences of childhood, we should journey to a place in nature that served as a power spot when we were young. These could be:

• A place you visited regularly to escape the tensions of family life.

• A very memorable place you went to only once, such as on a family vacation, but which took on mythic qualities for you such that you still remember in some detail the spot or what occurred there.

• A place you visited occasionally, such as a farm, the beach, or a place in a state park that was a favorite family picnic spot.

• A place you never actually visited but knew about that always held some haunting fascination for you, such as a nearby estate or the far side of a river.

These places of refuge might have served two purposes. For people whose family life was abusive and violent, the power spot may have been a place of hiding, an escape from a home life of fear and loneliness. For people whose childhoods were less traumatic, the power spot might have been sought out joyously from a healthy need to be alone, to engage in reverie, to daydream, to explore, to spend time with invisible companions. The spirit of either type of place may be helpful for your adult spiritual practice.

As in the journeys to the childhood companions, seek the spirit of place, in human or animal form, and ask it these questions:

• What have I forgotten about this place?

• Do you have any specific instruction about my current life or spiritual practice?

• Is there a place I should go to today for the same kind of spiritual renewal I used to find with you?

If it seems to be a spirit that will continue to play a role in your life, get to know it and learn in what ways it can be of help.

THE WORDLESS JOURNEY

We did not begin life with full-blown language. Words and their meanings, sentence structures, the subtlety of phrasing, all came slowly over the years with much practice and a good deal of frustration. Our earliest sense of oneness with the environment did not require words. In fact, using words, especially the naming of objects—"dog," "cat," "nose," "Daddy"—was part of the process of dismantling that oneness, of learning that we were individuals separate in some way from the rest of the universe.

Our first efforts at speech used language in a magical way. We chattered nonsense syllables to express some feeling in the presence of objects, people, and experiences. We may have coined secret names for things, long before we knew or could pronounce their real names. Four-year-olds playing in a room are constantly chattering, often to themselves, without any apparent attempt to communicate with their playmates. Observers have suggested that they are literally "talking out their worlds," creating their universe of experiences verbally as they perform them physically. Language here is totally expressive, magical, nonsensical, related primarily to the child's interior experience of what she or he is doing.

Tribal people, especially shamans, have similar personal ways of using language. Shamans understand the language of animals and birds, communicate with trees and rivers and mountains, and return from journeys to the spirit world with new power songs. Like children's singsong verses, shamanic practice includes chanting words, phrases, or simple vocables to achieve a nonordinary state of consciousness. Equally important is the shaman's ability to be quiet and relate to nature and the spirits without the intrusion of language, which tends to separate experience into categories, by words and names, and to structure experience artificially along grammatical lines.

Orpingalik, an Eskimo shaman, explained that our thoughts are driven by a force like a flood or the weather that prevents us from finding new ways to express ourselves, but then "an abatement in the weather" will occur. He continues:

[Then] we, who always think we are small, will feel still smaller. And we will fear to use words. But it will happen that the words that we need will come of themselves. When the words we want to use shoot up of themselves—we get a new song.[6]

Lame Deer said that his people find symbols and images to be a blend of the spiritual and the commonplace, unlike Westerners, for whom "symbols are just words." He explains:

To us they are part of nature, part of ourselves—the earth, the sun, the wind and the rain, stones, trees, animals, even little insects like ants and grasshoppers. We try to understand them not with the head but with the heart."[7]

We need to get our heads out of the way and overcome our insistence on using words with the linear limitations characteristic of adult communication. In general, adult speech is structured for predictability and control, to ensure that others will understand us correctly. As children we were taught that language should be used solely with other human beings (and possibly household pets), not with trees, toys, birds, or wild animals. We were taught to use words as adults used them. In brief, the child gives up its unique, magical, expressive way of talking so that speech reflects only ordinary reality. Unless, of course, the child becomes a poet.

Poetry retains the personal, expressive, mystical qualities of language; words and symbols need not reflect the agreed-upon definitions. Instead, they can reflect the poet's personal view of reality and do nothing other than express the poet's feelings of the moment. If others hear or read more into the poem than the poet intends, no harm is done. In fact, the world's great poetry bridges the realms of ordinary reality and the reader's own sense of the nonordinary realities hidden in his or her personal experience. The bridge itself is the poet's vision, captured in words no other has ever arranged in quite the same way.

Since words can be used in a more mystical way—for personal expression, for communicating with the spirits of nature, for inducing a dreamlike state of consciousness—our shamanic practice would benefit if we could turn off momentarily the normal course of word flow, Orpingalik's flood or weather, so that an abatement occurs in which we experience our journeys nonverbally, with only the heart to unite us with the spirits we encounter in the Otherworld. Like the Zen practitioner who strives to turn off the roof brain chatter flowing through the head, the shamanic practitioner can do journeys that halt the flow of worrisome, anxious, fretting thoughts that dominate our waking lives. You can structure a "wordless" journey this way:

1. Make the intention clear to your power animals and helping spirits that there will be no talking during the course of the journey.

2. Request your power animal to escort you without the use of words through the Otherworld or some particular location in the Otherworld that you select before the journey begins.

3. Any spirits encountered on the way will be treated silently.

4. What's even more important, and more difficult, is to also turn off your roof brain chatter. Whenever you catch yourself talking

to yourself about what is occurring on the journey, you must refocus on the wordless intent of the journey.

There is a simple way to handle these verbal distractions based on a method used in various forms of meditation.

1. When distracting thoughts—such as analysis, judgment, criticism, explanations—begin to flow through your mind, simply let them go and look directly at whatever is before you.

2. Then name it.

3. After naming it, go up to it, look at it very closely, and touch it. Hold your hands on it until the journey continues or something else catches your attention.

4. Notice where your power animal is and give some kind of nonverbal signal, such as nodding your head or stretching out your hand, that you want the journey to continue.

5. You might also experience Orpingalik's feeling of getting smaller, allowing the object you are touching to dominate your attention or loom up in your visual landscape.

Usually these techniques will silence your internal talk and allow the journey to continue of its own accord.

Richard Lewis, founder and director of The Touchstone Center for Children in New York City, relates, "It is through seeing and touching that we gain access to a language of feeling which rivets the attention on what things are. As children we do not know the names of things but their shapes, textures, and smells." Lewis recalls the insight of an eleven-year-old who told him, "A feeling thinks by seeing and touching."[8]

By focusing on seeing and touching you can discard unwanted verbalized thoughts, and the journey will continue. Do not be too judgmental about this or blame yourself too severely for analytical and critical distractions. Expect them to occur frequently because they are characteristic of our thinking in ordinary reality. Simply release them by seeing, touching, and naming the object, and then getting on with the journey. (We add "naming" to this process of handling distractions because it would be unrealistic to pretend that we do not know the names of things. Naming an unwanted thought is also taught as an effective method for handling distractions in some forms of meditation.)

Once again, the purpose is to explore and sense the landscape of the Otherworld somewhat as we did as children when we touched everything we could get our hands on, even putting most of it in our mouths.

FINDING A NEW SONG

There is a way to record the wordless journey that will allow you to find a new spirit song. (Actually, you can use this method to record any journey, but it works especially well with the wordless journey.) You will need a blank piece of paper with a circle about the size of a quarter drawn in the center of it.

1. Use only single words and short phrases to record the journey.

2. Scatter the images and events of your journey around the circle, placing the entries so that they are not in a linear format.

3. Avoid complete sentences. Instead of writing "I saw a rugged mountain," write simply "rugged mountain."

4. If you use a verb, add "ing" to make a gerund so that you avoid forming a sentence. For example, do not write "A fox ran up the hill," but "fox running up the hill." Instead of writing "I flew with Eagle," write "flying with Eagle." This use of the gerund will also keep the journey in the present tense, where it is more alive and immediate.

5. When you have finished recording all the sights, sounds, sensations, and events of the journey, look at them carefully, reading them over and over in different sequences to discover which three or four elements were the heart of the journey. Try to select the phrases that capture the essence of the journey.

6. Circle these three or four phrases.

7. Then using the imagery in these phrases (you need not be concerned about preserving the exact wording), combine them so they become a short, three-line, haiku-like poem. Think of this as a short poem that will bring back the major memories of the journey experience when you read it a week later. Then write that poem.

Use the haiku form as a model for these poems without being concerned about the technical requirements of syllables and themes that characterize genuine haiku. I always recall Beat poet and American Buddhist Jack Kerouac's definition of a haiku: "a very tiny poem." It helps to read a selection of haiku before doing this exercise just to get the feel of how short the lines are, how the lines need not be complete sentences, and how they unite only two or three of the poet's observations. Even though brief, the poem is an intense glimpse into a much larger and broader experience. Freed from the need to express the complete scope of the journey, you can use the three short lines to convey depth, which is a quality of the soul. Think of the poem as the soul's brief expression of what occurred on the journey.

After you have written the short poem, read it out loud repeatedly for a few minutes, listening for the natural rhythm contained within it. Eventually the poem will reveal its inherent cadences, which can be the groundwork for a chant or new song. Perhaps just one line will leap out at you, asking to be sung. If it does, sing it. Even if you claim not to be a poet and certainly not someone who can sing, you may be amazed at how easily the spirit song in your very tiny poem will "shoot up of itself." You will also be amazed at how good it is.

NURTURING THE SHAMAN IN YOUR CHILDREN

The natural shamanism of childhood does not survive intact into adulthood for cultural and societal reasons, but part of our practice can include discovering ways to encourage the spiritual lives of our own children so that, like tribal children, they might make a smoother transition into adulthood and not leave their earliest spiritual wisdom in the playpen. There are a number of ways for doing this.

DREAMING TOGETHER

Take your children's dreams seriously, especially nightmares. Even though your child cries out for you and needs reassurance that he or she is safe from the threatening features of the dream, resist the temptation to say that the dream "wasn't real." Dreams are real. And what they represent in the child is real. There are ways to help your child overcome frightening dreams. Take a child troubled by dreams on a hike to find a "dream stick." The stick can be carved or painted to suit the child and then taken to bed at night. The stick is empowered to give the child the ability to meet the fearsome creatures of the night and turn them into friends and allies. Tell your children that when they have another frightening dream, they can stop *in the dream* and confront the monster, asking it to be friendly and give them a gift. In time, children manage their dream lives so that they are not disturbed or frightened.

Even pleasant dreams need validation. In some tribes, family members routinely share dreams with each other in the morning, looking in the dream material for information about how to live the coming day or handle problems. It is important for children to know that you dream too, and know what you dream about. When they see you taking your nightly visions seriously, they will take theirs seriously too. A side benefit is that dream-sharing opens the doors of communication between children and adults.

JOURNEYING FOR POWER ANIMALS

A ten-year-old boy was hit on the head by a baseball bat and knocked unconscious. When he regained consciousness, he suffered vision impairment. As a shamanic practitioner, his mother organized a power animal retrieval ceremony with a few of her friends and some of her son's companions. The purpose was to retrieve a power animal with exceptionally good sight to reinforce on a spiritual level the work being done with eye doctors to restore her son's vision. They met Eagle. Eventually, the boy's vision returned to normal. But what's equally important is that the boy will forever have a memory of the spiritual work that was done for him in childhood, as well as a memory of his mother's personal involvement in his shamanic experiences as a child.

Power animal retrieval ceremonies can be used to lend a new dimension to a child's current problems. A first day at school, an illness, a sporting event or school competition, a stay in a hospital, even trips to the dentist can be occasions to find power animals for your children or to hold ceremonies to reconnect with power animals. The efforts will show results in their current lives and, what's more, create the memories of spiritual experiences woven into the ordinary events of their childhood, to be recalled later in adulthood.

You can journey for a power animal for your child, or, if your child seems mature enough, let him or her journey for the power animal. I have worked with children ten to sixteen years old and found that they can readily encounter a power animal even without doing a formal journey into the lower world. Here is a format for doing this with a group of children or one child.

1. Explain to the children that there are animal energies everywhere, even though we cannot always see or feel them. This means that animal spirits are capable of being anywhere too.

2. Discuss the fact that spirits are by nature invisible and inaudible to us under ordinary circumstances, so we need to prepare

places in our imaginations, or "imaginal realms," for them to make themselves known.

3. Explain to the children that spirits use images to communicate with us.

4. Have each child prepare a "spirit place" in his or her imagination by seeing (or sensing) a field. Ask each to create a woods at one end and a small hill somewhere in or near the field and to locate a body of water, such as a pond or stream, somewhere nearby. Have the children see their fields clearly with their eyes closed before you begin to drum. Have them use as many senses as they can to experience the fields.

5. Ask them to open their eyes and describe their fields to you.

6. Demonstrate the drumbeat and callback procedure.

7. Next explain the structure of the journey. Tell them that they will lie down and begin to see their fields as you start to drum. Explain that they will "go into" the fields and silently call out for their helping spirits to appear in the form of animals.

8. Give them some guidelines as presented in Chapter Two on how to recognize which animal is the power animal.

9. Explain that each child can communicate with the animal in any ways that feel natural and can ask the animal to display its powers, skills, and knowledge.

10. Encourage the children to hang out with their power animals until the drum signals that the journey is coming to an end.

11. Explain that they should say goodbye to their power animals, but that they will continue to feel the animals' presence in their daily lives.

12. Tell them that the journey can end by simply letting the field fade from their awareness, and by becoming conscious once again of the floor where they are lying in ordinary reality.

13. When the journey is over, teach the children some of the techniques in Chapter Two for maintaining contact with power animals.

RITES OF PASSAGES

Attention should be given to rites of passage at the time of puberty. A girl's first menstruation can be incorporated into a "Moon Ceremony" in which the mother and other women in the family or circle of friends welcome the young girl into the community of women. A boy's puberty rite may be harder to time since there is no one event that marks the boy's entry into manhood. But at some point, perhaps when he beings to shave or enters high school, the father along with other male friends and family members could take the boy camping, tell stories about manhood, share their own experiences, and use shamanic rituals and techniques to welcome the boy into the circle of men. Graduating from grade school or high school can also be events for shamanic ceremonies: to find power animals, to journey for help in making life transitions, and so on.

INVITATIONS TO ADULT CIRCLES

Allowing for the different rates that children mature, at some point you may want to include them in drumming circles (see Chapter Nine). This might coincide with a rite of passage. Occasionally participating in drumming circles might also be a way to keep the lines of communication open during adolescence. Most likely, the "normal" trend in our society for teenagers to have as little to do with parents as possible will win out over their interest in taking part in adult drumming circles, but it's possible that adolescents may view the shamanic practice of their parents as just offbeat enough to make it "cool" to some extent and they will want to take part now and then.

It is important in our culture for children to develop a healthy sense of self, separateness, and ego in order to survive in our society. Every parent will have to evaluate his or her children's needs and not allow the visionary life of the child to be used as an escape from learning the responsibilities of adulthood. Nevertheless, children are marvelously flexible, and we should probably not underestimate their ability to "walk in balance," keeping the worlds of ordinary and nonordinary reality separate and, with our help, staying focused on the distinct tasks of becoming an adult.

It's not easy to do this. As Laurens van der Post put it, "What people called growing up [is], in a measure, one of being educated out of reality, above all the great invisible realities which matter so much more to a young person than the physical ones by which men set by far a greater store as they grow older." [9] To become an adult in our culture may require this. On the other hand, for shamanic practitioners and their children, the break with the invisible realities may be less severe.

A few years ago I organized a power animal retrieval ceremony for fifteen eighth-graders who were on their graduation camping trip. We asked to meet power animals that would help the kids adjust to the many new and frightening changes they would encounter as they entered high school. When we were finished and picking up our drums and rattles, a young boy came up to me and announced proudly, "You know, I have more power animals than the Bear I met today." I showed surprise, and he listed several power animals: Cougar, Eagle, Mouse, and Squirrel. I asked how he found these power animals, and he answered, "My mother does this stuff!" It so happened that his mother belonged to a shamanic drumming circle and occasionally the members invited their children to join them. As I looked down at this young man, a strange thrill ran through my body. I was meeting the second generation of shamanic practitioners!

Core shamanic practice has only been available to mainstream Americans for about twenty years, but already we are witnessing the emergence of the next generation of practitioners. If we recall that Zen Buddhism has been widely accessible to Americans for only about three generations and already there is a recognizable style of American Zen Buddhism evolving, we should watch eagerly for the developments in core shamanism among the next generations of practitioners, as they and we develop a truly American form of core shamanic practice. In tribal cultures, older and younger shamans depend on one another to keep the traditions strong and vibrant. So should we.

◉ Chapter Eight

ANCESTRAL SPIRITS

Some years ago I visited a friend suffering from AIDS in the hospital. He looked gaunt, wasted, and on the verge of death, but his eyes were still bright and vital. He said, "I think there's still a lot of spirit inside me," and as I looked at him and sensed the energy around his emaciated body, I had to agree. "You have a lot of life in you," I offered. Then he asked me, "Would you drum so that it will leave?"

This was the first time I had been asked specifically as a shamanic practitioner (and a friend) to help someone die. My friend knew about drumming from our occasional journeying together over the years that we knew each other. He figured that I would agree to his request and left it up to me to work out the details of it. He didn't really care. He wanted to die and move on to the next world. I promised I would drum for him. I went home, took out my drum, and the feeling that I had never drummed before swept over me. I wasn't sure I knew how to do it.

I made a journey to ask for advice and was instructed simply to sit and drum and see what happens. So I began a practice of drumming almost every day until my friend finally passed on, about two weeks later. On some occasions I found myself journeying to the lower world to do whatever "tasks" I might be given to help his spirit move on; sometimes I journeyed through the middle world to his hospital room just to be with him; but usually I didn't journey at all. I just drummed, and the drum worked. He is now among the ancestors.

Shamans traditionally perform "psychopomp" services for the dying, a term from the Greek that means literally to "lead the soul" into the next world. An Irish woman, trained in shamanic techniques by her grandmother in the 1950s, explained:

> When a spirit is leaving this world and there's fear, I and other entities bring them as much light as we can. Pour light into them, just pour so much light into them…(that) the old fear doesn't have a prayer…(then) the individual that is going to make the trip between the two worlds just rises up into the light.[1]

Today shamanic practitioners are being called upon to do this same kind of work, now in settings and under circumstances far removed from the familiar village environment where for centuries shamans have helped men and women live their lives and meet their deaths. We have much to learn, and much to develop, if we hope our modern practice will be of the same service to our own families and friends in their last days as that performed by traditional shamans.

BEING WITH THE DEAD AND BEING DEAD

Historically shamans have had close relationships with the spirits of the dead. In some cultures the spirits of deceased relatives or tribal elders call the candidate to begin the training for shamanhood. Often the initiating spirit is the spirit of a deceased shaman. The Yakut shaman Tusput describes his initiation:

> One day when I was wandering in the mountains up there in the north, I stopped by a pile of wood to cook my food. I set fire to it. Now, a Tungus shaman was buried under the pyre. His spirit took possession of me.[2]

This spirit helped Tusput so intimately that during trance work Tusput spoke Tungusic words.

The great authority on world religions Mircea Eliade points out that in some cultures the souls of the dead "serve the candidate as a means of entering into contact with divine or semidivine beings (through ecstatic journeys to the sky and the underworld, etc.) or enable the future shaman to *share in the mode of being of the dead.*" [3] I emphasize this last statement because it expresses a widespread belief among many indigenous cultures, and yet it is not readily talked about among modern shamanic practitioners. Seldom do practitioners of shamanism consider themselves to be in some sense dead, by which I mean looser, freer, more detached from the physical world in order to be in closer conscious contact with other realities.

It's possible that this may be due to some essential difference between being a shaman as opposed to a shamanic practitioner, or it reflects some ingrained, contemporary attitude about death that modern practitioners acquire from society—an attitude that argues against the idea of a living person being in some ways dead. I opt for the latter explanation and encourage practitioners to explore and learn from their helping spirits ways to reclaim the more ancient notion and adapt it to their practice in whatever ways possible. Learn how to be in some ways dead. Doing so will increase your sense of being able to bridge the worlds of life and death and to function more effectively as a walker between the worlds of ordinary and nonordinary reality. It will also strengthen your confidence in speaking about death and preparing for your own.

The human spirit is free, independent, immortal, and capable of transcending any physical form in which it resides. Our current bodies are indeed only temporary. There were others before, and there will be others after we slip out of these physical shapes that we think we can't live without. As shamanic journeyers there are numerous bodies, life forms, and periods of time we can inhabit during the ecstatic soul flights of the shamanic journey. This is a primary reason for practicing core shamanism. The sixth-century Welsh bard and shaman Taliesin spoke of his many transformations into different animal and life forms as a kind of death. He said, and we can concur, "I have been dead, I have been alive...There is nothing in which I have not been."[4]

THE SHAMANIC JOURNEY AND THE NEAR-DEATH EXPERIENCE

Initiation into the shamanic journey is a paradigm of death, having many characteristics of the near-death experience (NDE) itself. Both the shamanic journey and the NDE are distinguished primarily by the tunnel that leads from the familiar surroundings of ordinary life into a lighted area that exists outside the matrix of physical space and time. A person who has a near-death experience (called an NDEer for convenience) is met by the spirits of departed family and friends who assure him or her that the journey into the next world will be safe when it is finally the person's right time. Like the shaman, the NDEer returns to ordinary reality, often with radically different attitudes toward life and death because of the NDE. For many returnees, the fear of death abates and they vow to live life more fully and altruistically on a daily basis. The NDEer is alive again but in a different and more profound way. The same is true of the shamanic journeyer.

A shaman in some way shares the status of the dead because he or she realizes the spirit-nature of human existence more consciously than others. Being able to journey through the invisible doorways between the worlds and return requires some element of noncorporeal existence similar to that which characterizes the dying as they leave their physical bodies. In some cultures shamans are considered dead while their spirits are separated from their bodies during the shamanic trance state, and they return to life when they re-enter ordinary consciousness.

The Eskimo shaman Aua told the explorer and ethnographer Knud Rasmussen of another reason why the shaman has a special relationship with the souls of the dead. Quite simply, the dead enjoy the shaman's visits. Aua said:

There is always great rejoicing in the Land of Day when a spir-it-conjurer [shaman] comes on a visit; immediately, all the souls of the dead come rushing out of their houses...They hurry toward the newcomer, glad to pay their respects, happy to make him welcome; for they believe that he is, like themselves, the soul of a dead man.

But when they realize that he is a shaman, not one of the newly departed, they are disappointed. But the shaman stays and

enjoy[s] himself for a while with the happy departed, [then] he returns to his companions in his home place, tired and out of breath. Then he recounts everything he has experienced.[5]

Again there is remarkable similarity between the reactions of the spirits Aua speaks of and those of the deceased family and friends who are happy and joyful in welcoming an NDEer into the next world and disappointed when the NDEer is told that it is not time yet and he or she must return to the land of the living.

But Aua tells us that the shaman can enjoy visits to the Land of Day and that spending time with the souls of the dead is beneficial both for shamans and, later, for the living who are instructed by the shamans' accounts of their journeys. Shamans are "geographers of death," discov-ering the thresholds into the next world, exploring its terrain, inform-ing the living about conditions there, and assuring them that although the dead live in the next world, they are not inaccessible. In these ways shamans bring comfort to the living, by bringing glimpses into the great and fearful questions about what awaits us after death and by remind-ing us that the worlds of the living and the dead are not totally discon-nected from each other. They assure us that communication continues across space and time, between the mysterious network of realities that form the universe. Most important, shamans remind their communities that it is possible to sojourn into the land of the dead and return.

The bodies of the dead and the places where they repose sometimes play vital roles in shamanic practices around the world. In Siberia, shamans save the skulls of elder shamans after they die and use them for divination. The simple technique is to ask a question of the deceased shaman, then lift the skull. If the skull feels light, the answer is yes; if the skull feels heavy, the answer is no. Eliade points out parallels between this practice and the Greek accounts of Orpheus, whose head served as an oracle after his death, and Norse stories about the skull of the god Mimir, which also gave advice to the living.[6]

Celtic legends are filled with accounts of severed heads, such as that of the Welsh leader Bran, continuing to talk and give instruction from the Otherworld. In Christian times the skulls of Celtic saints were often preserved in sacred places that became sites of pilgrimage where the devoted would seek advice. The Celts continue to make pilgrimages to the graves of Christian saints and the burial mounds of ancient gods and goddesses to experience a form of communion with the Otherworld and to receive inspiration from otherworldly beings.

THE DEAD TAKE US SERIOUSLY

Studies over the last twenty years have shown that the dead make spontaneous contact with former friends and family members on a surprisingly frequent basis. Anywhere from 47 percent to 67 percent of those widowed (both men and women) report spontaneous contacts with their departed spouses, some hearing their voices, others seeing them in their physical forms, a few even feeling their touch. Among the general public, from 25 percent to 42 percent report post-mortem contacts with someone they knew. Among parents who have lost a child, more than 70 percent claim to have had contact with their deceased children. Allowing for the fact that many people are afraid to admit such encounters with the dead for fear of not being taken seriously or being thought crazy, the figures might be even higher. Add to these statistics the eight million Americans who have had at least one NDE in which they met the spirits of departed acquaintances, and the number of people who have contact with the dead is very high. Virtually everyone reports that encounters with the dead are uplifting, encouraging, and bring a sense of peace and acceptance, reassuring the living that the departed are doing well.[7]

From these statistics it appears that the dead are maintaining contact with us, whether we are interested in doing so or not! Loving connections between people are not broken by the fact of physical death. Ordinary men and women continue their relationships with the departed even without formal skills in mediumship or shamanism. Some therapists encourage clients in mourning to maintain an active relationship with the deceased and to carry on dialogues with the spirits of loved ones in order to handle their grief and move on with their lives. The current thinking is contrary to the popular folk advice that usually runs, "Forget him, get over it, he's gone, get on with your life." It is through memory, reverence, and consciously honoring the departed that life for the living resumes its normalcy.

Shamanic practice prepares a person to conscientiously retain some contact with the departed. In fact, if we model our practice on the core traditions of indigenous shamanism, it virtually requires our having some kind of ongoing relationship with the dead. And who else would be a better personal advisor and counselor about both living and dying than someone we knew and whose judgment we respected while alive? Seeking spiritual advice and instruction from the spirits of those we knew and respected in this life should become part of our spiritual practice. The dead may become important otherworldly allies on a regular basis, or they may offer help in certain situations, such as when we are assisting the dying or preparing for our own deaths. Journeying to meet someone you knew in this life is possible because death does not totally sever the lines of love and communion that joined you in this world.

JOURNEYING TO DEPARTED ACQUAINTANCES

Not every deceased spirit is able or willing to reconnect with the living, although the experience of mediums and shamans is that many spirits, maybe most, are in a state that allows contact with the living to some extent. Here is a respectful approach for determining who among your deceased acquaintances might be the object of a shamanic journey.

• Take a few days, or even weeks, to reflect and meditate on who this person should be, especially if you have had several acquaintances pass away in recent years.

• You can ask the spirit of someone who has passed on to come to you in a dream or send you an omen if he or she wishes to be contacted. (See below about dreams and omens.)

• Or, you can do a journey to ask your power animal or other spirit instructors who among your deceased acquaintances would be a promising candidate.

A general practice in mediumship and spirit contact is not to try to contact the spirit of someone who has recently departed too soon after his or her death. The dead need time to arrive and adjust to their new lives. There are no agreed-upon lengths of time that should be honored, possibly because the entry into the next world is personal and individual. You might consult with your power animal and other spirit instructors about this, and consider your relationship with the deceased and what his or her wishes would probably be in the situation. If for some reason your candidate is not ready or able to communicate with you, you will be told.

When you have decided on the person to contact, choose one of the methods below for structuring the journey. This journey is not into the classic "Land of the Dead," which is often described in shamanic and mythological literature as a frightening and depressing realm, fraught with danger to the journeyer's well-being. The Land of the Dead is where confused spirits await their final transit from this life to the next, some not realizing they are dead, others still inordinately attached to this life and unable to let go. These are the people shamans and mediums traditionally help cross over to the other side. They are not the spirits you would want as guides and instructors, nor are they really capable of serving as such. If you discover in your preparatory journeys and reflections that the person you seek as a spirit guide is in this kind of condition or state, consult with your power animal about the possibility of doing psychopomp journeys to assist him or her in crossing over completely into the realm of glorified souls.

WHERE TO MEET AND WHAT TO DO

When planning to meet the deceased on a shamanic journey, you have several options.

• Most people report they have contact with the dead and other noncorporeal entities in the upper world. Have your power animal arrange a meeting for you at some location in the upper world with which you are already familiar, or ask it to take you to any pleasant meeting place that it selects for this purpose.

• You can also journey into the middle world to the spiritual dimension of a place where you and the deceased used to spend time together, such as a park, a beach, a garden, or some other place in nature that would be a familiar and comfortable place to visit. Even if the place is no longer in existence, your journey outside of space and time can take you back to a "spiritual reflection" of the original site that will serve as common ground where you both have imprinted your energies, where you have left spiritual footprints or shadows, as it were, and where you would both find it comfortable to be together again.

• You can also ask your power animal to take you to some specific type of place in the lower world, such as a field, meadow, parkland, beach, or some other spot that you ask to be prepared just the way you would like it so that you and the spirit you meet will feel comfortable.

In counseling people who have lost loved ones suddenly and who want to make a contact to say goodbye and complete unfinished business, I will teach them to journey through an opening into the earth and through a tunnel to a particular place that they decide upon before the journey begins. We spend some time deciding where this place will be, what it will look like, what season it will be, what plants or objects will be there, and so forth. This allows the newly trained journeyer to be taken to familiar surroundings without anxieties about what he or she will find. It is important not to have to worry about these things, since the primary goal of the journey is to spend time with the deceased, not explore an otherworldly landscape. One client whose teenage daughter had died in an automobile accident without him getting a chance to say goodbye to her chose to meet her near the tennis courts where they used to play together. To his surprise, when she appeared, it was not only to give him the opportunity to say goodbye, but to play a game of tennis. He didn't tell me who won.

Decide the goals of the meeting:

• One goal will be to experience what it is like to encounter the spirit of someone you may not have had contact with since he or she passed away. You will want to greet each other and renew your relationship.

• Ask the person any specific or personal questions, and be ready to answer questions that the spirit may ask you.

• Find out if the person will be available for regular meetings and to serve as a spirit instructor for your shamanic practice or to advise you on important life issues as they come up. If the answer is yes to these questions, then you can begin to develop an ongoing relationship with the person. If not, this may be your only meeting, and you will have to conclude your business on this journey.

• Assuming the person agrees to be an instructor or advisor, find out if there are any requirements or conditions for journeys to get together or if there are means of communication other than journeying, such as dreams, automatic writing, omens, and signs in nature.

• You can also ask if the person has a power animal or animal messenger that you should know about. This animal can be a sign from the person when you see it in ordinary reality. It can also be a power animal you can journey to in nonordinary reality that will be a messenger for the spirit or convey its instruction.

• You should ask if the person wants it known among other living acquaintances that he or she is working with you in this way. Respect the spirit's wishes on this.

• One of the benefits of having the spirit of the deceased as an instructor is learning about issues related to death, such as how to prepare for your own death or how to assist someone who is dying. As mentioned above, this information can be extremely valuable for shamanic practitioners called upon to be of assistance to the dying, especially in these times when people are greatly concerned that they leave this world in ways that are personally meaningful for them.

• Enjoy the encounter. Dance and sing with the person if this seems appropriate.

ANCESTRAL SHAMANS

Many shamanic practitioners who come from European ancestry or cultures that do not have a current shamanic tradition to draw upon often wonder if any of their forebears were shamans and what practices they engaged in. From fairy tales and folk magic we can discern the vestiges of older shamanic customs—shapeshifting, healing with spells, herbs, and incantations, having intelligent animal companions, journeying to nonordinary realms within the earth or above the sky—but we cannot always be certain just how these feats were performed.

Since ancestral knowledge is never totally lost—all things that have ever happened are imprinted somewhere in the spiritual realms of the universe—we can journey to the spirit of an ancestral shaman to learn the old ways that were part of one's family or cultural heritage. This is similar to journeying to the deceased and can be orchestrated much like journeying to meet someone more recently departed. A variation, however, is to journey back in time to witness the tribal or peasant life of your distant kinfolk and to seek out a shaman or spiritual healer to ask for instruction.

Whatever information you are given should be brought back with respect and with the sincere intention of continued study and reflection as you put it into practice. Not every custom or technique from ancient days is appropriate for the modern world. For example, most tribal peoples practiced animal sacrifice and in some eras, even human sacrifice—practices that today would violate our sense of ethics and morality, even though earlier ages believed in them deeply and sincerely and felt they were necessary. Furthermore, the average man and woman of centuries past was physically conditioned to withstand a more rigorous asceticism that we today would find unbearable and even dangerous to our physical or mental health. The herbs, stones, woods, and other natural ingredients used for medicines centuries ago may not be available today or might have a harmful effect on modern people.

Whatever advice you receive from ancestral spirits should be carefully evaluated by both you and your other spirit instructors, as well as by other shamanic practitioners whose judgment you respect. Nevertheless, general principles, inspiration, and personal stories from ancestral instructors can be invaluable in rooting your shamanic practice in the spiritual heritage from which your family comes. You may discover methods of night vigils, vision quest techniques, ancestral deities, tutelary spirits, or clan totems. As part of your academic practice, read and study in the folklore, history, and anthropology of the people you descend from to become as well informed as possible.

SPIRIT DREAMS

The dead frequently appear to us in dreams. Not every dream that contains a deceased figure, however, is necessarily an important message or encounter. As with dreams in general, we need to distinguish between what some cultures call "big" dreams and "little" dreams—those that are truly significant and those that seem to merely recycle the events or worries of the preceding day. Usually a reliable indicator that you have had a "big" dream is that it leaves you with a powerful tingly sensation or a sense of heightened stimulation upon waking, a disquieting feeling that the dream was important. When you have a big dream about the dead, you may want to work with it shamanically to unravel its further meanings and applications for your life.

Equally helpful are dreams about the deceased that you incubate. Dream incubation, or programming, is the practice of giving yourself suggestions during the day and immediately before falling asleep at night to dream about a certain subject. In this case, you would ask the spirit of a deceased friend to come to you in a dream. Many people need to make this request for several nights in a row before the dream occurs. This might be necessary because the spirit is waiting to see how urgently you really desire the dream, or possibly to give your suggestions time to clear out other distractions from your dreaming mind and prepare it to receive a dream about the intended subject.

A respectable theory about incubated dreams, although one that is not accepted by everyone, is that when you ask for a dream on a particular subject, then whatever you dream that night is about that subject, even though the subject may not be literally apparent in the manifest content of the dream. This theory argues that the dream's intended subject is concealed in metaphors that ask the dreamer to go deeper into the dream and spend more time to unlock the dream's message than would be necessary if the manifest content of the dream were clearly about the requested subject. For our purposes, if you ask a spirit to come to you in a dream or give you instructions about some matter in a dream, then whatever you dream about that night should be interpreted as relevant information from or about the deceased spirit.

Whichever way you choose to understand incubated dreams, here is a method for journeying into a dream to explore more fully its message and meaning. In Chapter Nine there is a method for using this dream-journey technique with a group.

• You can begin at the beginning of the dream and go directly through it as it occurred.

• Or ask your power animal to take you back into the dream wherever it thinks you should re-enter it.

• Ask explicitly to re-enter the dream at a specific point that holds some interest for you.

• Everything in the dream can communicate with you, so you can ask people, animals, places, and objects why they are in the dream.

• You can also ask your power animal the significance of any person, place, or object in the dream.

• Three questions that can be asked of anything in the dream and that usually produce relevant information are: Why are you in my dream? What gift/power/advice can you give me for my life today? Are you really something else, something other than what you appear to be in this dream?

• You can also go to any point in the dream and change it, allowing the dream to unfold in different ways than it did when you dreamed it. For example, if there is a point in the dream where you were just about to go through a doorway and didn't, now is the chance to do so, accompanied by your power animal. If there was a figure in the dream you wanted to approach or question, now you can.

• You can extend the dream beyond the point where it ended. Most dreams "break off" or fade out without coming to a real conclusion. In the journey you can dream the dream further and find out what happens next.

• Similarly you can "back up" and explore the events immediately leading up to the point where the dream began.

If the spirit of the deceased appeared clearly and conveyed meaningful information to you, this redreaming journey is not necessary. But if the dream had a mysterious or inexplicable quality, or the spirit did not appear but you are nevertheless accepting the dream as having come from the spirit, then journey into it as described.

SIGNS, SECRETS, AND SYNCHRONICITIES

Jim, a friend whom I have known since high school and college, died unexpectedly while undergoing a lung operation. A few years later I was driving alone in my car, listening to an "oldies" station, when a 1960s song came on that was a favorite of Jim's, a song by the Shirelles, one of the popular "girl groups" of that decade. For no apparent reason I had the urge to say, "This one's for you, Jim," and I began to sing along out loud. That started something. Now whenever I hear a Shirelles's song (and I'm alone in the car), I sing along for Jim.

A month or two after I started this practice, I pulled a book off a shelf to look up some bit of information, a book I had not used in years. When I opened it, out fell an old Christmas card from Jim dated 1988, several years before he died. There was nothing remarkable about it, no poignant message or picture, no special handwritten note other than "Hope the New Year is a good one." There was no reason for me to have saved it, so I assumed I had used it as a bookmark, sticking it in the book nearly eight years earlier and then forgetting it. Almost immediately I realized why it came tumbling out when it did. It was a sign from Jim that he hears and appreciates my gigs with the Shirelles.

The dead are with us in subtle and not-so-subtle ways, often nudging us out of the trances induced by everyday life so that we wake up to their presence in our lives. Signs and synchronicities, such as Jim's faded Christmas card, occur more frequently than we realize because we tend to miss them altogether or dismiss them as oddball coincidences. But they are more than quirks. A synchronicity is a *meaningful* coincidence, one that leaps out at us, makes us tingle, conveys a sense that some other intelligence is involved in our daily activities. The spirits use synchronicities to keep us mindful of their continuing life in the next world and to keep their spirits alive in this world, especially in our minds and hearts. Rather than rely on our ability to retain old memories, they give us these current events so that we know they are still around.

People engaged in regular spiritual work, such as meditation, prayer, and devotional practices, tend either to have synchronicities more frequently than others or to notice them more often, possibly because spiritual activities condition a person to be more alert to subtle, nonphysical influences in daily life. As mentioned earlier, if you keep a journal of synchronicities, you will become aware of their frequency.

Signs and omens from the dead can take several forms. As in the case of the old Christmas card, a sign might be one of a kind and marked in some clear way that it is from a specific person (a friend's signature is pretty clear!). Other signs might be one-of-a-kind but not so obvious. But if the event has a tinge of importance about it, you probably should assume that it is a sign from a deceased friend. A journey to your power animal or another spirit instructor later can confirm the synchronicity or explain it more clearly.

You can also journey to the deceased to request signs. One way to do this is to ask, "What should I accept as a sign from you?" This is similar to asking to know a deceased friend's power animal. You might be told that certain times of the day are more receptive to signs and omens, such as sunsets and sunrises, which are betwixt-and-between times conducive to spirit influence. Or you might be told that the nights of the full moon are times when a particular spirit will contact you. The presence of certain birds or a bird acting in a certain way or appearing at an auspicious time might be a sign. The dead may want you to go to certain places—perhaps ones that were important to them while they were alive—to receive signs. Maybe key dates in the lives of the dead are times to receive signs, omens, or dreams.

As with dreams, not every coincidence is necessarily an important message or sign from the deceased. You may be told that the cardinal is the totem of a deceased relative, for instance, but not every appearance of a cardinal is necessarily a greeting from the deceased. By being alert, reflecting on the times and places that cardinals appear to you, by noting the significance of events, and by asking for interior assurances from the deceased, you will become more skilled at interpreting signs and omens.

GRAVESIDE RITUALS

Visiting graves goes in and out of favor. It was a popular pastime in the nineteenth century, as was the landscaping and architecture of cemeteries. People had picnics at graves, and tombstone statuary and mausoleum design competed with statuary and architecture found on the landed estates of the wealthy. In the mid-twentieth century, many people found this morbid, and visiting graves was relegated mostly to Memorial Day. Americans found other places to have picnics. But shamanic practitioners have valid reasons for visiting the final resting places of the dead that transcend current fad, and following are some of them.

• *Sleeping on graves:* Among indigenous people in Siberia and Australia, among the Eskimo in the Arctic, and among the Celts, sleeping at or on the grave of the dead helped facilitate communion with departed friends and acquaintances. The belief that the souls or spirits of the dead remain near their bodies varies from place to place, but such a belief is not necessary for engaging in the practice. The spirit is not bound by time and place; it transcends time and place. But the grave may hold some imprint that is helpful for the living to make contact with the dead. Regardless of one's belief, the grave is simply a logical spot for initiating contact, as it is for holding rituals to honor the dead.

The practice of night vigils and vision quests important to shamanism everywhere can be arranged at the grave of a helping spirit if the graveyard is accessible at night. Most large public cemeteries are closed at night, but often smaller cemeteries near the local churchyard are open. While it is not advisable to sneak into a graveyard after hours, when it is closed to the public, you might get special permission by inquiring with the director if certain arrangements could be made for an overnight vigil, especially if you put it in the context of a spiritual practice to honor the departed.

• *Journeying at the graveside:* You can journey shamanically to the deceased while at the graveside, if the area is private and secluded enough that you feel safe to do so. If not, simply drum or rattle at the grave to call the spirit of the departed more intimately into your conscious awareness. The deceased recognize our efforts to make contact with them and to keep their spirits alive in memory and ritual, so visits to the graveside for these activities do not go unnoticed or unappreciated in the spirit world.

• *Grave-tending:* Grave-tending can be an important activity for honoring the dead: mowing grass, planting flowers or shrubs, placing seasonal decorations such as wreaths or flags on the grave. You can enhance ordinary grave-tending practices by incorporating them into some of the activities listed below.

Leaving gifts: It is customary in many cultures to leave gifts such as flowers or food at the grave. As part of a shamanic practice that includes the dead as spirit helpers, we can leave sacred objects such as crystals, stones, and carved sticks.

Spreading our ashes: We can burn ritual herbs or incense and leave the ashes on the grave.

Create a graveside circle: We can honor the grave as the center of a sacred circle by invoking the four directions or by burying crystals or power objects in each of the four directions around the grave. We can also plant special herbs or shrubs in each of those directions.

Sharing soil: It is an old folk practice to take home a small amount of topsoil from the grave to use in rituals, keep on an altar (similar to preserving ashes), or sprinkle on the flower beds or lawns of other members of the family. This practice can include sprinkling a small amount of soil from your own home on the grave of the dead, signifying the exchange of love and energy that continues to flow between you. The amount of soil need only be a handful or spoonful, since quantity is not important but rather the intention and the presence of some physical thing associated with the deceased. (Keep this in mind when removing topsoil from a grave; shoveling up bucketfuls of soil might be construed by local authorities as an attempt at grave-robbing or desecration.)

Shamans journey into nonordinary reality to maintain the ancient bonds of kinship with nature, the elements, and the dead. Ancestral wisdom can fuel our spiritual journeys through life, and by tapping into that reservoir of knowledge through the help of the spirits of the deceased, we become more spiritually connected with the greater universe. We should celebrate the dead with song and dance, just as we do power animals and the spirits of nature and the seasons. In ecstatic dance or journeys outside of ordinary consciousness, we participate in that free and fluid state that the dead enjoy. In some sense, then, we are dead, if only while we revitalize our spirits by merging with the greater flow of energy and divine power in nonordinary reality. In so doing we gain insight into what the deceased already know: that we are both alive and dead, and there is nothing in which we cannot be.

 Chapter Nine

DRUMMING GROUPS AND JOURNEY IDEAS

Making the shamanic journey your core spiritual practice requires that you incorporate it regularly into your life. You can drum and journey alone or with others, for the intentions discussed in the preceding chapters or for other reasons that you discover as your spiritual life unfolds. Often ordinary life as well as the visionary life found in dreams, synchronicities, and journeys inspire us with ideas for shamanic journeys. This chapter provides guidelines for forming and conducting group drumming circles and ideas for various journeys.

DRUMMING CIRCLES

GENERAL GUIDELINES

The *membership of a drumming group* should consist of mutually compatible people who like and get along with one another. One of the most commonplace problems with spiritual groups is dissension and personality clashes. While all interpersonal problems cannot be avoided, it helps the group get through difficult times of controversy and hurt feelings when people trust and respect each other.

Selecting new members for a drumming group should be done carefully. If you plan to form a drumming group, begin with one or two friends with whom you feel comfortable. After meeting for a while you may decide to enlarge the group, so the core members should work out a process of selection or invitation. One way to do this is to let any of the core members suggest a new participant who then would meet once or twice with the group to allow the others to meet him or her. This would give potential new members a chance to scope out the group as well and decide if it is doing the kind of spiritual work that they are looking for.

Later you can hold a selection discussion and a vote to see if the new candidate is acceptable. Determine guidelines ahead of time as to what kind of vote will admit new members, such as simple majority or unanimous. You may also decide to give the new member a period of probation after which the established members would decide if continued participation is desired.

How often to meet should be mutually agreed upon. Many groups find that meeting once a month is not sufficient. If a person has to miss, it is a long two months between sessions. Once a week is probably ideal, but it can become too much of a commitment for many people. So meeting twice a month or every three weeks seems to be a good practice.

Some groups also choose to meet at the important seasonal changes: the two equinoxes and two solstices, adding perhaps the old pagan holidays that fall between these points: February 1 (Imbolc), May 1 (Beltane), August 1 (Lammas), and November 1 (Samhain). These sessions can be in addition to the regularly scheduled meetings or in place of the one that falls closest to the holiday.

Meeting on the same night of the week is a help in remembering. When the night varies from week to week or month to month, it is easy to forget. However, if the group cannot find some regularly convenient night each time, then it is good to schedule the meetings in advance for two or three months so members can reserve those nights.

The role of group facilitator can fall to one individual or rotate among the members. The facilitator can be responsible for beginning the session and seeing that the discussion about what kind of journeying to do (see the sample format below) runs smoothly. The facilitator can be some individual other than the person who hosts the sessions in his or her home.

A SAMPLE SESSION FORMAT

The group should decide as a whole on the general format for the meetings: what time to meet, length of sessions, how many journeys to do, what kinds of journeys, and other ritual activities such as creating sacred space, chanting, dancing, sharing journeys, and so forth.

Following is a sample format:

Create sacred space by placing a candle in the middle of the floor, perhaps on a small blanket to create a central focus or altar. Members can place some of their own sacred or ritual objects near the candle. Sit on the floor in a circle around the candle with drums and rattles.

Burn herbs or incense and pass the container around the circle to let members bless and purify themselves. This is called smudging in Native American traditions.

Engage in about five to ten minutes of group drumming/rattling. Shamanic drumming should be done in unison so that the drumbeat and rattling create a mesmerizing effect to begin the process of altering consciousness. Avoid "free" drumming or rattling that produces a cacophony of competing beats. The goal is to produce a sound that is unifying and consciousness-shifting.

When finished, one member of the groups calls the spirits from the four directions (or invokes the four directions) with a rattle. This can be done nonverbally by simply rattling in each of the directions, or the invoker can use some simple formula as described in Chapter Three. The role of invoker can rotate from session to session, with each person using the formula that appeals to him or her; or the group can compose a formula for invoking the spirits that is used each time.

The invoker should also honor the sky and earth by rattling overhead and down near the floor.

Last, the invoker should rattle for a few moments over the head of each person in the circle to acknowledge each one and his or her power animals and other helping spirits.

When the invoker sits back down in the circle, hold hands for a few minutes of silent reflection. A song or chant can be sung to end the period of silence.

The facilitator then initiates the discussion that precedes the actual journeywork. This can be done by letting each member update the others on what has transpired in his or her life since the last meeting. Or the facilitator can ask if anyone in the circle has some special need or interest for the group to address in the evening's work. Although the group may be meeting primarily as a spiritual community, it is not out of place to do healing work as well.

At this point the group should decide what the evening's journeys will be about. If the journeys are short—about ten to fifteen minutes— there is usually time (and energy) for two. Occasionally the group may decide to do one long journey of a half hour or more. When two journeys are done, you might let the first journey be for each individual's personal intentions and the second journey have a common purpose. Or the first journey can have a common purpose, and let the theme of the second journey evolve out of the first.

When the purpose of the journeys has been determined, dance your power animals. This can be done with drums and rattles, although every member does not need to have one. Select someone to be responsible for setting the beat and ending the dance. If you wish to circle around the candle, decide on which direction you will move to minimize the chances of people running into each other. People can also, of course, dance in place. Dancing power animals can last as long as the group decides. Ten minutes is a good minimum length of time, but you may wish to dance longer since dancing deepens the shamanic state of consciousness for journeying.

When the drumbeat signals the end of the dancing, everyone lies down on the floor to journey, except the person who will drum, who can either stand or sit in the middle by the candle. The drummer may want to say a few words after the others lie down, suggesting that they take a few deep breaths and relax and reminding them of the purpose of the journey.

The signal to return from the journey developed and used by the Foundation for Shamanic Studies consists of a sharp, brief break in the drumming, followed by four drum rolls of seven beats, thirty to forty-five seconds of very rapid drumming, and then four more drum rolls of seven beats. This usually gives everyone time to end the journey and return to ordinary consciousness.

In a small group the drummer can see that everyone is beginning to stir and return to ordinary awareness. However, it is a good practice for the drummer to ask in a quiet voice if everyone "is back." Anyone who has not had time to finish the journey and return can give a hand signal, and the drummer can continue drumming softly near that person until he or she returns.

Allow time for each person to return to a more ordinary state of consciousness and record the journey or make notes in a journal. Then those who wish may share their journeys with the group.

When the sharing and discussion are complete, begin and conclude the second journey in the same manner.

The evening's meeting can be closed in several ways. You can rattle in the four directions again to acknowledge and thank the spirits for joining the circle. Or the group can join hands and someone can offer a prayer, blessing, or song to close the session.

JOURNEY IDEAS

Shamanic journeying as a spiritual practice does not rule out other healing, counseling, decision-making, and life-planning types of journeys, but the focus is more directly on spiritual development, enlightenment, and the search for wisdom. Put another way, we journey to explore the Greater Universe, to discover its inner workings and attune ourselves to the flow of Life. We hope to learn more about the metaphysical laws and patterns that underlie the cosmos and to discover ways to serve others and the planet as a whole.

THE REDREAMING JOURNEY

Earlier cultures believed that divine messages came to us in dreams, and one of the spiritual services performed by shamans and spiritual leaders was to help dreamers understand the meaning of their dreams. The redreaming journey can be done by yourself to explore the possible meanings of a dream (as explained in Chapter Eight), or it can be used by a group in which everyone helps the dreamer unravel the hidden messages within the dream.

Redreaming a dream as a group practice is done in the following way. (The inspiration for this journeywork comes from Montague Ullman's excellent book *Working with Dreams*.) The dreamer tells his or her dream to the group twice—once to let everyone hear it told as a story, then again a bit more slowly so that others can make notes or outline it. If the dream is short, taking notes is not necessary, but the dreamer should still tell the dream twice so that everyone grasps the essential parts.

Next, the others may ask the dreamer "clarifying questions." These are questions to "see" the details of the dream more clearly and accurately. They are not "interpretive questions." Clarifying questions are similar to the following: You said there were a lot of people in the room—about how many? You said it began to rain—was it a shower or thunderstorm? You said you saw a man walking down the street—was he young, old, tall, short, or what? Can you describe him? You said you went into a dark room—how dark was it? Pitch black or dimly lit?

Interpretive questions should not be asked at this point in the process—How do you feel about your mother being in the dream? What do you think the runaway horse in your dream means? How would you describe your relationship to your daughter? In other words, the participants do not want any clues as to how the dreamer might interpret the dream or what he or she presently thinks is the meaning of the dream. Knowing this kind of information can interfere with the redreaming process.

The object of the journey is for each person *to adopt the dream as if it were his or her own, not the dreamer's*, and to journey into it similarly as if redreaming a dream of his or her own along the guidelines given in Chapter Eight. In other words, from the moment your power animal takes you back into the dream, at whatever point you would like to begin, you are seeking information about the dream *as if it were your own*. This is very important. *You are not journeying to find out what the dream means for the dreamer, but what it would mean if you had originally dreamed it.* If you see the dreamer in your journey, ignore him or her. Do not engage in dialogue or interaction with the dreamer because doing so deprives you of the fullest experience of making this dream your own.

So if the dreamer's mother, sister, or friend is in the dream, you must see your own mother, sister, or friend. If you do not have a sister, then ask your power animal to let you meet a spirit figure who will function as a sister in the journey. It is not uncommon in dreams to have a sibling who does not correspond to any member of the dreamer's family. More common perhaps is dreaming that we live in a house that does not look anything like our actual house.

After the journey ends, write down the journey with the greatest amount of detail that you can. Then each person shares his or her journey, speaking as if the dream in the journey were his or her own. Be sure to include in your telling both what happened and how you felt. Feelings are a key component in dreams and are often overlooked. During the sharing process, the speaker should not look at, address, or engage the dreamer directly. In fact, let the dreamer sit back and take notes on what he or she is hearing.

Hearing other people discuss your dream can be remarkably exciting and enlightening. The other journeyers create a rich potpourri of possibilities to shed light on the meaning of the dream. As the dreamer listens to them, he or she will sift through the details, occasionally being startled by how accurately someone's journey or part of someone's journey rings true. Even hearing a journey that seems "wrong" or inappropriate to the original dream can be enlightening because the process of discovering the meaning of a dream includes being certain what it does *not* mean.

I recall an instance in which the dreamer, who was thinking of moving to join a spiritual community in North Carolina, dreamed that she was being smothered by responsibilities and personal obligations where she currently lived. She feared that the dream was telling her not to move but to stay where she was. A man in the group journeyed into her dream and discovered that for him this was precisely the message: Don't move to North Carolina. But when he articulated it out loud, she knew immediately that this was not the meaning of her dream. Everything in her recoiled from the idea of not moving to a new home in North Carolina. She knew that moving was the right decision and that the dream was about something else. In the process of hearing others in the group share their journeys, she found other possibilities about what the dream was saying. Ultimately she realized from the others' experiences that the dream was mainly telling her to take time to finish up her affairs and discharge as many obligations as possible before she moved.

The dreamer also journeys back into the dream but does not share this journey until the others in the group are finished telling their own. Then the dreamer shares his or her journey. Finally the dreamer tells the group what he or she currently feels to be the meaning (or meanings) of the dream, and what details from the others' journeys helped the dreamer come to this conclusion.

THE HEAD OF WISDOM JOURNEY

In the Celtic tradition the head of a person who was revered in life as one of great wisdom or holiness was preserved as a relic or established as a place of pilgrimage. In both pagan and Christian eras, preserved heads or skulls of powerful or saintly figures continue to impart wisdom and counsel to those who seek it. In our own lives we have "gone through" several or many heads. Like snakes that slough off their skins each year, we slough off heads as we grow older. These heads and the wisdom they contain are not lost, but like everything that has ever happened, is happening, or will happen, they are preserved in the timeless and spaceless realms of nonordinary reality. This is a journey back to a former head to ask for advice about some current problem or issue in your spiritual life.

For example, many practitioners of core shamanism have left behind some or all of their former religious training and spiritual beliefs. For some there are continuing conflicts or tensions over this, either in terms of lingering guilt for having left the religious tradition of their parents or psychological/spiritual problems engendered by abusive or shaming practices in the former religion. Some people, on the other hand, sincerely seek to recover or renew some of their former beliefs and integrate them into their shamanic practice.

This journey is to ask your power animal to take you to a place in nonordinary reality where a previous head now resides, one that you feel could provide counsel or instruction in these kinds of matters. Of course, you can journey to a former head for nonspiritual questions as well, such as questions concerning relationships, career choices, insights into adolescence to help you understand your own children, and so forth. Following are some examples of how to use this journey for spiritual growth.

If you gave up formal religious practice when you were twenty-five and now feel guilty about it, journey back to the head you had at that age and ask to understand more fully the reasons for that decision. If you had a great spiritual devotion at age eighteen, and you would like to rekindle that spirit in your current practice, journey to your eighteen-year-old head and ask it what you are forgetting about spiritual fervor. Journey to a head you had during a period when you had no spiritual practice or beliefs, and explain to it why you practice shamanism; then ask it for advice on how you might deepen and strengthen your practice.

When your power animal takes you to a former head, you can interact in two ways. You can speak directly to the head as you would any other spirit figure on a journey. Or pick the head up, turn it around, and place it over your current head like a mask. Then ask the questions, or walk around in the journey and let the head inform you by simply letting you rethink and remember the old times that you wish to re-explore. Remove the head before returning to ordinary reality and place it back where you found it.

THE GRAIL QUESTIONS JOURNEY

The story of the Grail Quest has so many variations and interpretations that to search for the correct or original one is probably futile. But the power of the Grail lies not so much in its discovery as in the questing, for ultimately the search is for the Self and the Meaning of Life most important to the searcher.

Briefly, and at its most basic, the story involves the adventures of a good-hearted youth or knight who, while bungling through multiple escapades, stumbles upon a mysterious castle where a lame or wounded king resides. The kingdom also suffers because the waters of life no longer flow up from the nourishing springs and wells. The king rules over a wasteland. That evening at the king's banquet, the youth witnesses a procession of beautiful women in which one carries the sacred Grail and another a bleeding lance. Out of shyness or politeness, the youth refrains from asking three questions that intrigue him: Whom does the Grail serve? Why does the lance bleed? What do these wonders mean?

The next morning the youth awakes to discover the castle, the wounded king, and the maidens have all vanished. He must begin his quest again. But on the way a wise old woman scolds him, saying that if he had asked those questions, the king and the wasteland would have been healed. The boy continues his search, eventually finds the king and Grail castle again, this time asks the three questions, and the king and his kingdom are restored.

Taking the cue that there is something inherently healing and restorative in asking these three questions, we can construct a journey that will begin to heal and restore our spiritual life. Since the Grail quest is primarily a quest for the Self and the Meaning of Life, we can ask the Grail questions about our lives: Whom does my life serve? Why does my life bleed? What does my life mean?

The answers to these questions are inherently spiritual, for each casts its own light upon the path of the soul. The first reminds us that our spiritual practice should not be self-serving, even though spiritual development and enlightenment motivate us. We have responsibilities to others and to the planet.

The second provides insight into the inevitable suffering of human existence and encourages us to look beyond the sorrow with faith that it has some greater significance.

The third casts us into the very heart of all spiritual mysteries, the ultimate meaning for our incarnation in this time and place: What does my life mean?

We can approach these questions in the spirit of the Grail story, mindful of the old woman's remark that simply asking the questions is beneficial. We don't need answers. She reminds us that to live within the questions, to embrace the mysteries, to find security in uncertainty is the way of the seeker, and that we must continue to be seekers, no matter what answers we find along the way.

Decide who among your helping spirits you should journey to with these questions, then go to them and ask the Grail questions as they pertain to your life. You may want to reserve each question for a particular spirit counselor, or ask all three of the one you think might best answer them. If the spirits decline to answer one or more of the questions, accept that for the time being. It may be that you are not meant to know all the answers just now. You can repeat this journey later. In fact, this is a good journey to do periodically, whenever your life takes a new direction or when you are troubled by something. Be mindful that it is not necessary to receive answers, but simply ask the questions. Asking the question, accepting the mystery, begins the soul's healing.

DIVINATION JOURNEY

The word *divination* means literally to discover the divine will or the divine messages that can inform our lives. Every culture has methods of divination, from reading the signs and omens in nature, to casting lots, to scrying, or "seeing" signs in substances such as crystal, water, smoke, or clouds. Tarot cards, rune stones, and the *I Ching* are popular forms of divination in our culture.

For shamanic practitioners who are in regular communication with the spirit world through journeys, divination is an ongoing process. The more that we are able to ignore our own agendas and wishes while journeying, the more receptive we are to undiluted and undistorted information from the realm of spirit. The journey itself is the method of divination. Depending on the reliability of our spirit helpers and the quality of the information they give us, we can serve others as diviners.

Every life issue or question can be viewed as spiritual, or as having spiritual implications, no matter how mundane or materialistic it might appear. For that reason, the term *divination* in its original sense is not inappropriate for the process of seeking information about buying a house, falling in love, changing careers, or what to do about your health. The shamanic journey can be and is used to bring back information on these kinds of issues. However, practitioners who make shamanism a spiritual path will find ways to use the journey method to enrich their spiritual practice and to assist others in their own search for spiritual knowledge and wisdom.

When others ask you to do a divination journey for them, spend some time deciding with the person how the question should be worded. In general, avoid yes-or-no questions because there are simpler and faster divination methods for this, such as using a pendulum, drawing a card, or tossing a coin. Instead, take the *issue* of the question and ask for more information because information is precisely what the shamanic journey so wonderfully provides. Ask "what" or "how" questions, such as What do I need to do (to make something happen)? How can I (make something happen)? What will my life be like if I (do such and such)?

One should also avoid "why" questions because there may be many reasons for a problem, and knowing one or even all of them may not be any real help in solving it. Just knowing why does not provide a plan of action. Instead of why, ask "how" or "in what ways" you can solve the problem. You may be surprised how often the journey will spontaneously provide insights into the reasons why.

After you and the seeker have decided on the question, write it down. It's good to repeat it to yourself three times before going through your entry into the lower world. When you meet up with your power animal, tell it that you are journeying for so-and-so and that this is her or his question. State the question to your power animal just as it is written. From that moment on, whatever your power animal says or does should be considered relevant information for the seeker. You can always repeat the question as the journey proceeds just to stay focused if necessary, especially if you think the journey is not providing relevant information. But bear in mind that you may not realize in the course of the journey what is and is not relevant.

The important point when doing divination for someone else is that you do not need to know what any of the information means. You are the messenger, not the interpreter of the message. Your responsibility is to carry back information, not interpret it. When you return to ordinary reality, share the journey in every detail with the seeker, no matter how irrelevant or off the point some of it may seem to you. To the seeker the very piece of information you may be inclined to dismiss as being of little value may hold the key to providing an answer for the entire problem.

Always let the seeker decide what the journey means, but part of the session might include the two of you discussing different ways the journey, or parts of it, might be interpreted. One way to get at the heart of a journey in which the content seems obscure in relation to the issue is to ask the seeker (or perhaps the seeker will ask you), "If you had to summarize the advice given in this journey in one brief sentence, what would it be?" Often, forcing yourself to reach some conclusion about the bottom-line meaning of the journey is one way to elucidate its significance.

POWER ANIMAL RETRIEVAL

As part of your shamanic service for others, you can use your practice to introduce other people to the notion of animal spirits as guides and guardians. As we have seen in earlier chapters, you may have friends and family members who could benefit from knowing who their power animals are, how to maintain relationships with them, and how to call upon them for help in daily life.

For a full description of a power animal retrieval ceremony, see Michael Harner's *The Way of the Shaman*, where he explains in detail a method for retrieving a power animal for another person.[1] As you practice shamanism, you will develop your own healing ceremonies for others based on methods such as Harner's and those you learn from other teachers. In brief, the power animal retrieval journey aims to bring back a power animal that will help another individual in some specific context, such as the young boy we saw in Chapter Seven who needed an animal to help him overcome a physical injury.

The journey begins with you lying next to the person so that your ankles, hips, and shoulders touch. (You will need a third person to drum for you, or use a drumming tape.) Then journey to the lower world and ask your own power animal to introduce you to the appropriate power animal for the person you want to help. When you meet the other's power animal, spend a few moments acknowledging it and thanking it for appearing. Tell it the reason that the person needs a power animal and ask if it has any advice it would like you to convey to the person. When you have gotten to know it, pull it in toward your chest, and let its spirit ride within you as you return to ordinary reality. Then get up and kneel next to the person. Bend over cupping your hands above the person's chest, and blow the power animal forcefully into the heart area. Next raise the person to a sitting position, and cup your hands over his or her head, and blow the animal in at that point.

Then, as Harner suggests, pick up a rattle and shake it around the person to seal in the spirit energy.

Tell the person what the animal is and share any messages it gave you. It's important to educate the person about the significance of power animals, how to honor them in daily life, call upon them when needed, deepen the relationship, and so forth. You can use the methods discussed in Chapter Two for this. The best method, of course, is to teach the person how to journey so that he or she can spend time in nonordinary reality with the animal spirit.

WHEEL OF THE YEAR JOURNEYS

Many individuals and drumming groups like to journey at the traditional turning points on the Wheel of the Year, often in conjunction with a seasonal ceremony honoring the changes taking place in nature at those times. The solstices and equinoxes, as well as cross-quarter holidays, make up the eight major spokes of change on the Wheel. Journeying can take a couple of approaches.

You can journey to the spirit of the season, asking to understand or experience what changes are occurring. Often this kind of journey takes you into the deeper regions of the earth, soil, waters, or winds to have a firsthand look at the energies and life cycles involved.

Another approach is to ask power animals or the seasonal spirits to give you a task to perform in nonordinary reality that will assist in the changes. By doing the task you put your own spirit energy into the season and help the Wheel turn. As part of the task or immediately following it, you can dance and celebrate the seasonal change before returning to ordinary reality.

A third method is to journey to ask what kind of work or ritual you can do in ordinary reality at this time of year. The instructions you are given may be for you alone or for a drumming group to perform. It might be something very ordinary such as plant a garden, take more walks, look at the stars at night before going to bed. Or it might have the nature of ritual or ceremonial activity.

If everyone in the group journeys on this topic to discover a group ritual, then share and collate the information, creating a ritual or common work task based collectively on as many as possible of the major ideas that the group brings back. Don't feel you need to incorporate everything; select those ideas that will make the best ritual or task.

INTENSIVE SHAPESHIFTING JOURNEY

Often on journeys we merge with power animals or helping spirits for part or all of the journey. This can happen spontaneously, or we might ask for it on specific journeys. Here is a longer procedure, verging on a ceremonial process, to intensify the shapeshifting experience and to acquire deeper knowledge of what it means to be some other spirit form. Since one of our goals in a spiritual practice is to realize our inherent oneness with all things and to remove the illusions that make us think we are separate, isolated beings, intensive shapeshifting journeys can be of great importance.

If you are working alone, use a drumming tape for the actual journey phase or have someone drum for you. You will also have to approximate the times for beginning and ending the different stages. About ten to fifteen minutes for each stage is suggested, although if you are working alone, you might decide to spend longer, letting each phase move into the next whenever it seems ready to do so.

There are three stages of preparing for the journey, the journey itself, then a special way of recording the journey that is discussed in Chapter Eight in the section about the Wordless Journey method. The following instructions assume that you merge with a power animal, but you can merge with any helping spirit who gives you permission to do so. You may want to spend a few moments before you begin, using a rattle to alter consciousness, and check in with the spirit or power animal with whom you wish to merge to see if it is appropriate to do so at this time.

Stage one: Lie on the floor holding a rattle. Bend your arm at the elbow so that the rattle is off the floor and you can shake it. Shake the rattle, and begin *thinking about the power animal* you intend to merge with. The sound of the rattle is a "head" sound, and the focus in this stage is to engage your thinking mind so that it concentrates exclusively on the power animal. Think about it, visualize it, imagine all you know about the animal.

Stage two: Without breaking your state of consciousness from stage one, sit up and drum in a soft heartbeat rhythm (or simply sit if someone else is drumming). Slow your breathing down a bit, and take deep, full breaths and empty your lungs more completely than you usually do. This will help keep your awareness in your chest and heart area. Let the *feelings or emotions you associate with your animal fill your heart and chest.* The drumbeat is a "chest/heart" sound and the focus here is to feel your animal's energy and presence in your heart as deeply as possible.

Stage three: Again without breaking consciousness, stand up and, using a drum or rattle, dance your power animal, *placing your attention throughout your body, but primarily in the lower belly, hips, and legs.* Dancing calls attention to the body and its capacity for physical activity. Become aware of how your power animal's energy fills your entire body now and directs the dancing by letting its spirit move within you.

Each of these three stages engages a different area of consciousness: mind, heart, and body. If each stage lasts about fifteen minutes, the entire process should take about forty-five minutes.

The journey: In a group, the leader sounds the signal that the dancing is concluded and immediately goes into the journey drumbeat. Drop to the floor where you are and *begin journeying as your power animal.* You may not need to formally go through your entry and tunnel if you already feel like the journeying began while dancing. Some people experience the journey beginning while they dance, but if you don't, go immediately through your entry and down the tunnel. By this time you should be fully merged or shapeshifted into the power animal, so you do not need to call it to join you.

The purpose of the journey is to learn how that animal experiences joy. You might call this journey "Coyote's Joy," "Raven's Joy," or "Swan's Joy" to honor your particular power animal. To the extent that your awareness has shapeshifted, you will probably not be able to discern what thoughts, feelings, and experiences are yours and which are your power animal's. You will be your power animal. Allow its spirit to journey through you, going about the activities in its life where it finds joy, delight, fulfillment of its natural capacities. As in the Wordless Journey, you will not need to engage in much conversation with your power animal, and to whatever extent you can, try to refrain from your normal human ruminations that can detract from the shapeshifted state of consciousness. When the drumbeat calls you back, disengage, separate, thank your power animal, and return to ordinary consciousness.

Recording the journey: As in the Wordless Journey, record words, phrases, and images on a sheet of paper that has a quarter-size circle in the center. Scatter these entries haphazardly so that the journey is not recorded in a logical, linear fashion. You can cluster related experiences near one another as you recall them, but refrain from giving the journey a prose-like narrative.

Then circle the four or five most vivid or memorable entries from the journey, the ones that hold the essence of the journey, and compose a short three- or four-line poem with them or with some variation on the experiences they express. Think of this poem as having the title "Coyote's Joy" or whatever your power animal happens to be. Let the poem become a song in some way, by looking for the natural cadences and patterns in the wording, or by taking one or two lines and chanting them to an appropriate drumbeat, or by dancing this poem and letting the rhythms that emerge suggest a melody. Use the song/poem over the next few days to recall the journey and weave the experience into your daily life.

EPILOGUE

We embark upon a spiritual practice because we seek the meaning of our lives within the mysteries of the universe. And when we place ourselves within the mysteries, we must be prepared to have great faith, great doubt, and great determination. Any spiritual practice involves all three because the practitioner is searching through the darkness of life, looking for the light that leads to our True Home.

But we are not searching alone, for as shamans in every culture reassure us, the cosmos abounds with help. All created things are alive, conscious, and want to communicate. The Creator has endowed all creatures with wisdom and joy, and they are eager to share with us their ways of being in the world. In time we learn to recognize them as our companions.

An old Celtic prayer to bless someone leaving on a journey reminds the person that

> You are the pure love of the clouds,
> You are the pure love of the skies,
> You are the pure love of the stars,
> You are the pure love of the moon,
> You are the pure love of the sun,
> You are the pure love of the heavens,
> You are the pure love of each living creature,
> You are the pure love of the Creator of all life.[1]

Surely these are great companions to accompany us on our journeys.

NOTES

PREFACE

1. Joan Halifax, *Shamanic Voices: A Survey of Visionary Narratives* (New York: E. P. Dutton, 1979), 113–120.

CHAPTER ONE

1. Hal Zina Bennett, "From the Heart of the Andes: An Interview with Q'ero Shaman Americo Yabar," in *Shaman's Drum* (no. 36, Fall 1994), 45.

2. David Suzuki and Peter Knudtson, *Wisdom of the Elders: Honoring Sacred Native Visions of Nature* (New York: Bantam Books, 1992), 16–18.

3. Joseph Campbell, *The Way of the Animal Powers: Volume I* (San Francisco: Harper & Row, 1983), 169.

CHAPTER TWO

1. Joseph Epes Brown, ed., *The Sacred Pipe: Black Elk's Account of the Seven Rites of the Oglala Sioux* (New York: Penguin Books, 1971), 44–46.

2. Michael Harner, *The Way of the Shaman: A Guide to Power and Healing* (New York: Bantam Books, 1982), 84–86.

CHAPTER THREE

1. Halifax, *Shamanic Voices*, 38.
2. Halifax, *Shamanic Voices*, 61.
3. Mircea Eliade, *Shamanism: Archaic Techniques of Ecstasy* (Princeton: Princeton University Press, 1964), 39.
4. Harner, *The Way of the Shaman*, 39.
5. Carlos Castaneda, *The Teachings of Don Juan: A Yaqui Way of Knowledge* (New York: Pocket Books, 1976), 115.
6. Eliade, *Shamanism*, 129–136.
7. Holger Kalweit, *Dreamtime and Inner Space: The World of the Shaman* (Boston: Shambhala, 1988), 44.
8. Kalweit, *Dreamtime and Inner Space*, 36–37.
9. Kalweit, *Dreamtime and Inner Space*, 31.

CHAPTER FOUR

1. Donald Sander, *Navaho Symbols of Healing* (New York: Harcourt Brace Jovanovich, 1979), vii.
2. Sander, *Navaho Symbols of Healing*, 64.
3. Alexander Carmichael, *Carmina Gadelica: Hymns and Incantations* (Hudson, NY: Lindisfarne Press, 1992), 217.
4. Christopher Bamford and William Parker Marsh, *Celtic Christianity: Ecology and Holiness* (Hudson, NY: Lindisfarne Press, 1982), 49.
5. Halifax, *Shamanic Voices*, 251.
6. John G. Neihardt, *Black Elk Speaks* (New York: Pocket Books, 1975), 165.

CHAPTER FIVE

1. Suzuki and Knudtson, *Wisdom of the Elders*, 102.
2. Halifax, *Shamanic Voices*, 70.
3. Neihardt, *Black Elk Speaks*, 279–280.
4. Suzuki and Knudtson, *Wisdom of the Elders*, 108.

5. Gary Snyder, *The Practice of the Wild* (San Francisco: North Point Press, 1990), 109.

6. Halifax, *Shamanic Voices*, 37.

7. A. E. (George Russell), *The Candle of Vision: Inner Worlds of the Imagination* (Dorset, England: Prism Press, 1990), 3.

8. Carmichael, *Carmina Gadelica*, 411.

9. Esther de Waal, *Every Earthly Blessing: Celebrating a Spirituality of Creation* (Ann Arbor: Servant Publications, 1992), 16.

10. Carmichael, *Carmina Gadelica*, 267.

CHAPTER SIX

1. Suzuki and Knudtson, *Wisdom of the Elders*, 57.

2. James A. Swan, ed., *The Power of Place: Sacred Ground in Natural and Human Environments* (Wheaton, IL: Quest Books, 1991), 68–72.

3. Halifax, *Shamanic Voices*, 69.

CHAPTER SEVEN

1. Bennett, "From the Heart of the Andes," 44.

2. Kalweit, *Dreamtime and Inner Space*, 248.

3. Jean Liedloff, *The Continuum Concept: Allowing Human Nature to Work Successfully* (Reading, MA: Addison-Wesley Publishing Company, 1992), 107.

4. Henry David Thoreau, *Walden, or Life in the Woods* (New York: Signet Classic, 1960), 71.

5. O. Fred Donaldson, *Playing by Heart: The Vision and Practice of Belonging* (Deerfield Beach, FL: Health Communications, Inc., 1993), 48.

6. Kalweit, *Dreamtime and Inner Space*, 144.

7. John Lame Deer and Richard Erdoes, *Lame Deer: Seeker of Visions* (New York: Pocket Books, 1972), 96–97.

8. Richard Lewis, "Making a Language of Childhood," in *Parabola* (August 1995), 27.

9. Donaldson, *Playing by Heart*, 48.

CHAPTER EIGHT

1. Eliot Cowan, "Interview with an Irish Shaman," in *Shamanism: Quarterly of the Foundation for Shamanic Studies* (Summer 1992), 17.
2. Eliade, *Shamanism*, 82.
3. Eliade, *Shamanism*, 85.
4. John Matthews, *Taliesin: Shamanism and the Bardic Mysteries in Britain and Ireland* (London: The Aquarian Press, 1991), 319, 297.
5. Holger Kalweit, *Shamans, Healers, and Medicine Men* (Boston: Shambhala, 1992), 130.
6. Eliade, *Shamanism*, 391.
7. D. Scott Rogo, "Spontaneous Contact with the Dead: Perspectives from Grief Counseling, Sociology, and Parapsychology," in *What Survives? Contemporary Explorations of Life After Death*, ed. Gary Doore (Los Angeles: Jeremy P. Tarcher, Inc., 1990), 76ff.

CHAPTER NINE

1. Harner, *The Way of the Shaman*, 98–109.

EPILOGUE

1. Carmichael, *Carmina Gadelica*, 247, 264.

meeting allies in the, 64-66 Four elements:
drumming between, 99; and middle–world
journeys, 95-97, 99, 107-10; power objects
representing, 75; and sacred horizons,
59,67-72, 75-76; and sacred sites, 126

G

Grail questions journey, 196-97
Graveside rituals, 184-86

H

Head of wisdom (Severed Head) journey, 79,
173, 194-96
Hermitages, 128
Hopi Indians, 83. *See also* Native Americans
Horizons, sacred, xi, 59-84; in art, 79-80; and
the circle and the cross, 82-84; and families
of spirits, 77-79; and the four directions,
59, 62-66, 66-67; and the four elements,
59, 70-72, 75; of power and blessing, 59-62;
and the shamanic calendar, 80-82; and tal-
ismans/power objects, 72-76

I

Intensive shapeshifting journeys, 202-4

J

Journeys, x, 40-58; to departed acquaintances,
174-76; divination, 198-200; and drumming, 50-51; exploring your entry and
tunnel for, 44-45; finding your entry for,
42-43; and getting lost in the Otherworld,
56-58; grail questions, 196-97; ideas for,
191-204; intensive shapeshifting, 202-4;
and near–death experiences, 171-73; for
power animals, 33-34, 200-201; redreaming, 181-82, 192-94; Severed Head (head
of wisdom), 79, 173, 194-96; and the
shamanic state of consciousness, 44-48;
upper–world, 52-54, 56; what to do on the
first journey, 51-52; wheel of the year,
201-2; wordless, 156-60, 202, 204.

See also Lower–world journeys;
Middle–world journeys

K

Koyukon people, 112-13
!Kung shaman, 42

L

Ley lines, 133-35
Lower–world journeys: and discovering
tunnels, 43-44; entries into, 41-42; your
first journey, 48-52; summary of, 55

M

Middle–world journeys, 85-111; and breathing, 95-96; discovering, 86-89; and finding
our true nature, 110-11; and the four elements, 95-96, 107-10; indoors/outdoors,
99-100; and invitations and refusals, 101-3;
and journeying betwixt and between, 91-98;
and local and cosmic spirits, 100-101; and
prayers to spirits, 107-10; reasons for
doing, 89-91; and taking instruction from
the spirits of nature, 105-7

N

Native Americans, 57, 91; and ancestral spirits,
171-72, 184; and childhood, 140, 147, 157;
and the circle and the cross, symbolism of,
82-83; and drumming, 189; Emergence
Myth among, 60; and "medicine bundles,"
73, 74; and power animals, 26; and sacred
horizons, 60-61, 66, 73, 74, 79; and sacred
sites, 112-13, 122, 124, 133, 136.
See also specific groups
Navajo Indians, 60-61, 66, 67, 79, 82.
See also Native Americans
Near–death experiences (NDEs), 171-73
Night vigils: meeting power animals through,
28-30; and sacred sites, 136, 137-38
Norse tribes, 53

P

Q

R

S

T

V

W

Y

Z

Psychic Healing with Spirit Guides and Angels
by Diane Stein

A step-by-step guide to hands-on and psychic healing, this book presents a complete program of soul development for self-healing, healing with others, and Earth healing. Many of the methods included in his book have never before been published. Advanced skills include healing karma and past lives, soul retrieval, releasing entities and spirit attachments, and understanding and aiding the death process.

$18.95 • Paper • 0-89594-807-9

Essential Reiki: A Complete Guide to an Ancient Healing Art
By Diane Stein

Written from the perspective that Reiki healing belongs to everyone, this book differs from anything available on the subject. While no book can replace the directly received Reiki attunements, *Essential Reiki* provides everything else that the healer, practitioner, and the teacher of this system needs, including full information on all three degrees of Reiki, most of it in print for the first time.

"Stein's book is very detailed on every aspect of Reiki, from its ancient history to the hand treatment positions, the emotional causes of illness, giving treatments, and the initiations." —*NAPRA Review*

$18.95 · Paper · 0-89594-736-6

The Healing Energy of Your Hands
By Michael Bradford

This book has been specifically designed as an easy-to-read training manual to demystify the art of healing. The techniques described are so simple that anyone, even a child, can begin to sense and work with healing energy. The author's intention is that anyone using this book can, regardless of their educational or religious background or prior understanding of energy, awaken their own natural healing talents quickly and easily.

$12.95 • Paper • 0-89594-781-1

The Healing Voice: Traditional & Contemporary Toning, Chanting and Singing
By Joy Gardner Gordon

"If you didn't know you needed a book on this subject, browsing this one will convince you...Written gracefully and authoritatively *The Healing Voice* should appeal to those interested in New Age thought, healing, Eastern and native American religions, and music." –Booklist

$12.95 • Paper • 0-89594-571-1